VALUES AND THE CURRICULUM

Woburn Education Series

General Series Editor: Professor Peter Gordon

For over twenty years this series on the history, development and policy of education, under the distinguished editorship of Peter Gordon, has been evolving into a comprehensive and balanced survey of important trends in teaching and educational policy. The series is intended to reflect the changing nature of education in present-day society. The books are divided into four sections – educational policy studies, educational practice, the history of education and social history – and reflect the continuing interest in this area.

For a full series listing, please visit our website: www.woburnpress.com

History of Education
The Victorian School Manager: A Study in the Management of Education 1800–1902
Peter Gordon

Selection for Secondary Education
Peter Gordon

The Study of Education: Inaugural Lectures
Volume I: Early and Modern
Volume II: The Last Decade
Volume III: The Changing Scene
Volume IV: End of an Era?
edited by Peter Gordon

History of Education: the Making of a Discipline
edited by Peter Gordon and Richard Szreter

Educating the Respectable: A Study of Fleet Road Board School, Hampstead, 1879–1903
W.E. Marsden

In History and in Education: Essays Presented to Peter Gordon
edited by Richard Aldrich

An Anglo-Welsh Teaching Dynasty: the Adams Family from the 1840s to the 1930s
W.E. Marsden

Dictionary of British Educationists
Richard Aldrich and Peter Gordon

Biographical Dictionary of North American and European Educationists
Peter Gordon and Richard Aldrich

VALUES AND THE CURRICULUM

Edited by

JO CAIRNS, ROY GARDNER
and DENIS LAWTON

Institute of Education, London

WOBURN PRESS
LONDON • PORTLAND, OR

First published in 2000 in Great Britain by
WOBURN PRESS
Newbury House
900 Eastern Avenue
London IG2 7HH

and in the United States of America by
WOBURN PRESS
c/o ISBS
5824 N.E. Hassalo Street
Portland, Oregon 97213-3644

Website: www.woburnpress.com

British Library Cataloguing in Publication Data

Values and the curriculum. – (The Woburn education series)
1. Education – Aims and objectives –Great Britain
2. Curriculum planning – Moral and ethical aspects – Great
Britain 3. Curriculum evaluation – Great Britain 4. Values –
Great Britain 5. Great Britain – Moral conditions
I. Cairns, Josephine M. II. Gardner, Roy III. Lawton, Denis,
1931
370.1´0941

ISBN 0-7130-0222-0 (cloth)
ISBN 0-7130-4044-0 (paper)
ISSN 1462-2076

Library of Congress Cataloging-in-Publication Data

A catalog record for this book is available
from the Library of Congress

Printed in Great Britain by
MPG Books Ltd, Bodmin, Cornwall

CONTENTS

Part I:

The Challenge of Education in Values and the
National Curriculum in the Twenty-First Century

FRAMEWORKS FOR EDUCATION IN VALUES

Jo Cairns, Roy Gardner and Denis Lawton

The title of this book, 'Values and the Curriculum', may lead the reader to expect that the text will focus solely on primary and secondary schools and the content and process of the education provided. This would be inappropriate, since all educational institutions provide curricula, whether they are primary, secondary or tertiary. There are within the papers in the book many which are devoted solely to the compulsory age phases of the education system but these discussions of values, and education in values, could best be seen as examples of the issues that arise in all educational programmes.

The closing decades of the twentieth century saw significant changes in thinking about the nature of the societies in which we live, and a radical movement away from the certainties of life which provided stability and reassurance for earlier generations of both adults and young people. The broad spread of uncertainty has led to the disappearance of confidence built upon all pervasive belief systems, allowing for opportunities to explore a range of alternative interpretations of life and living in the world of late modernity as the new millennium begins. This shift from cultures of certainty to those of uncertainty has resulted from a number of factors which Giddens (1990) has summarised as:

- the global availability of information and sources of understanding
- instability of our knowledge bases as a result of the increasing pace of change in the world, through improved communication and technology

- greater international travel and exchange, bringing different belief systems into contact
- a strengthening of the link between social research and development, which has an accelerating impact on the societies in which we live.

All these factors have a noteworthy impact on the schools and other educational institutions which as children and adults we attend. The speed of change has rendered our knowledge bases fragile and our ways of organising knowledge, in the personal and public domains, open to continual question and mutation. Schools have suffered:

> the decline of the Judaeo-Christian tradition as the prime purpose underpinning schooling and teaching in a context of greater religious, cultural and ethnic diversity raises penetrating questions about the moral purposes of education. One of the greatest educational crises of the postmodern age is the collapse of the common school: a school tied to the community and having a clear sense of the social and moral values it should instill. (Hargreaves, 1994, p. 58)

Hargreaves continues to argue that the response of schools to this decline has been to search for statements to reflect the mission and the vision of each school, to express the raison d'être of the school and the strategies and processes adopted in whole school development and change. The school has had to seek a clearly expressed identity which justified not only its existence but also the particular contribution it seeks to make to the development of its charges and the community it serves. In this, despite identifiable generalities in school statements, the uniqueness of each school, so often paid lip service to in the past, has a clear expression. In this also the school becomes more readily associated with particular educational provision and more easily accountable to all concerned with its provision. The growth in the role of school governors, the majority of whom are from the immediate community, has ensured that the directions of change within the school are those which are of direct interest to the school community and that the school adheres to the directions, being accountable for both success and under-achievement in reaching agreed goals. In this mix of purposes, intentions, directions, frameworks and actions, the values the school espouses have a central place and provide lodestones to guide change and growth. With each institution seeking to define more precisely these values, there is more than ample scope for the expression of the individualism which lies at the core of the post-modernist movement.

This expectation of the reinvention of each school and its visible expression has taken time and energy and it is hardly surprising that, parallel with it, there have been attempts to define generalities which could be used to guide mission statements. Ungoed-Thomas (1997) has suggested a definition of a good school:

> A good school is one which successfully reflects in its teaching and learning the qualities of respect for persons, truth, justice and responsibility. These first virtues of education are both ends in themselves and means towards delivering the aims of the school. Any school which neglects the moral and subcultural virtues is poorly placed to help students develop as a whole person spiritually, morally, socially, culturally, aesthetically, mentally and physically. The practice of the educational virtues is a necessary condition for the achievement of all educational goods, whether utilitarian or didactic. (pp. 154–5)

The school has the responsibility of converting these rather general thoughts into focused statements on which to base day-by-day decisions about operational concerns. Many schools may find these thoughts to be imprecise and not reflective of their own individual circumstances. All schools should try to develop the whole person and, through the organisation of the school timetable, to provide for all those aspects of the individual listed in the above quote. In fact the school is required to do so by the national curriculum. However, some schools may feel that the qualities detailed are inadequate and do not meet the identified role of their individual communities. In this, schools which clearly profess a particular faith would be likely to insist on including qualities which have a religious focus. Whilst religious education is formally required by schools, there is evidence (vide Wintersgill, below) that in many schools, especially secondary, students are given only a limited exposure to this area of study. The defining of the nature of an educational institution engages the attention and resources of all and it must be asked if the energies devoted to it are wholly justified. However, Cairns (below) with Bryk (1993) has reminded us that we live through our institutions and it is the quality of those bodies which contribute to the fabric of society and the way we live our lives.

The demand is for all to participate in weaving the current plural and diverse community of the UK into a learning society, providing equal access and opportunity together with quality of learning for all, at all levels in the educational system. All the demands which are expressed require the stimulation of the social, economic, moral and spiritual values which underpin this national focus on learning. If learning gets to the heart of what it is to be human, as Senge (1992) suggests, then we need to examine these values in order to identify the kind of human beings national educational processes are working to develop. This concern is therefore about identifying the values present in practical policies, institutions, curricula and post-16 learning opportunities and their modes of delivery. Will current forms of learning enable active engagement with contemporary experiences and challenge conceptions of what it means to be human as we move through the new millennium?

The Archbishop of Canterbury (below) has drawn our attention to the need of everyone for *a moral language* and for society itself to have a moral language, if society is to be civilised, just and peaceful. He argues that working for the common good cannot be based on the reticence, embarrassment and incoherent mumbling which characterises much of the discussion of morals and values in Western society today. Dr Carey supports Jonathan Sacks in identifying extreme libertarianism as much the enemy of liberty as is anti-libertarianism and despotism. 'Without values such as trust, honesty, consideration for other people, love of justice and peace, there can be no liberty, because there can be no orderly society within which individuals can grow and express themselves in interdependence with others' (p. 18). However, Dr Carey has noted the recent emergence of the demands for standards within society and, in reviewing the work of the Nolan Committee, identifies the elaboration of Codes of conduct in public life as an indication of the desirability and the possibility of establishing agreed standards to which all should adhere. Dr Carey reflects that there exists within British society ample evidence of moral commitment in all walks of life, through the participation of many in public life, in the support given to dependent relatives, in the increasing focus on environmental and animal rights issues, and in the continuing interest in forms of spiritual exploration. This suggests there is a substantial bedrock of commitment on which society can build in a wide range of areas, including education but not depending exclusively upon it. For society to continue on a basis of support and justice requires institutions which espouse moral values, which can receive general acclaim. It would be totally unrealistic to expect schools to provide by themselves the moral guidance and set the standards of behaviour expected in society at large. Each institution, each person, has a role to play in developing the moral society and without that personal identification under a set of values Dr Carey argues that society could descend into disunity and anarchy. However, hope may be sought in the successes that SCAA (now QCA) had in gaining agreement by all faith leaders in providing The National Forum for Values in Education and the Community (1996). Perhaps this may be viewed as a starting point for the focusing of discussion on common values, which can be reinforced in educational situations through the provision for spiritual, moral, social and cultural development.

Schools are institutions which have urgent agendas: there are students to teach today and tomorrow, and schools cannot wait for the emergence of new thinking about how they should go about their business. Researchers and key thinkers on education seek to observe trends and to guide the steps that might be taken by schools and educational agencies. Lawton (below) has taken a radical view of the curriculum for the compulsory period of schooling. He has recalled his earlier analysis (1996) of school culture at these levels: behaviour (including the visible agents of curriculum, pedagogy and assessment) as part of the surface culture (or ethos); fundamental beliefs being part of the deep structure of culture; with attitudes and values somewhere in between the surface and deep cultures, and overlapping both. Lawton regrets how these cultures, translated in school practices, can create contradictions at each level. Eliminating these contradictions may not be easy and may challenge any number of daily practices within the school.

On analysing the existing curriculum structure, Lawton notes a number of assumptions he considers to be false and goes on to comment on the emphasis placed on the subject-based structure of the curriculum and the content and memorisation. He proposes a reorientation from content and objectives to skills and processes, and uses the Cognitive Acceleration through Science Education (CASE) project as an exemplar to suggest how the reorientation could be carried through into practice. In similar vein Lawton suggests a move from subjects and cognitive attainment to cross-curricular themes and the affective domain. Pupils who have studied the ten subjects of the national curriculum may be unable to cope with real-life problems which involve an understanding of their own society, including its political structure, and are unable to cope with questions of values and morality. He concludes that there is a need for a dramatic shift in the direction of social and moral education. Lawton also reminds us of a need to bring academic and vocational education closer together and joins with Pring (1995) in asserting the desirability of integrating both aspects of the learning experience.

The school curriculum is but one aspect of the educational scene and all would acknowledge the central role that teachers play in the conduct of the education of the students. What is of importance is the time available for teachers to carry out their functions, which include not only contact with their pupils but a range of administrative duties which are exacting and demanding. Hargreaves (1994) has stressed the growing gap between school managers and teachers, with increasing pressures being imposed by the managers for the school to reach agreed targets and objects. Hargreaves argues (p. 112) that the securing of non-contact time may have been at the sacrifice of how teachers can use such breathing spaces for professional purposes. He argues (p. 114) for the acknowledgment of what time means for teachers and for giving time back to the teachers, both qualitatively as well as quantitatively. Teachers should be given educationally substantial things to do with their time. This plea for a recognition of the way demands are made on teachers' time suggests the difficulties that teachers may experience in contributing to school development and, in particular, to the broader issues of schools' culture or ethos. Given the energies needed for good classroom practice, teachers may find it difficult to carry through into practice the standards for the Award of Qualified Teachers Status (TTA, 1997) which sets the agenda for the contribution of teachers to education values. The teachers:

• plan opportunities to contribute to pupils' personal, spiritual, moral, social and cultural development

• set high expectations for pupils' behaviour, establishing and maintaining a good standard of discipline through well-focused teaching and through positive and productive relationships

• set a good example to the pupils they teach, through their presentation and their personal and professional conduct.

Whilst the expectations are laudable, and an appropriate expression of the potential contribution of the teachers to values, we may be sympathetic and understanding of teachers who do not see them as easily achievable. Given the lack of clarity on what constitutes good teaching of values teachers might be excused if, in the order of priorities in the complex of teaching, education in values comes somewhat lower down the scale than elaborating strategies and materials which directly address subject specifications. As Taylor (below) has concluded, our aims in the field of values are unclear, and education in values is not yet a clearly identified curricular or culture-based process.

This is not to suggest that the inculcation of values should be marginalised and Pring (below) argues strongly that the teaching of values should be undertaken seriously. However this does not imply the promoting of one set of values which might be limited to a style of living, a particular community or to an uncharted set of guidelines propounded by social or religious leaders. Pring calls for the acceptance of *reasonableness* as a basis for helping the emerging adult to define relationships to be entered into, the selected lifestyle, the process for the resolution of conflicts, the recognition of individual worth and the value to be placed on objects and activities. The teacher and the pupil live in the same physical space but live in different intellectual worlds characterised by greater or lesser degrees of maturity and sophistication. In this, the daily turmoil of the classroom, there is little time to be spent on the exploration of values in an academic sense but there is time which must be used to every advantage to bring together the teacher and the child in the development of a valuing ethos which will guide the young persons to make appropriate choices for their future lives. Pring rejects the view that the values one holds are 'subjective' or a 'matter of taste'. He recognises the diversity of values but argues for the use of reasoning drawing upon debate, increased awareness and enrichment of experiences to provide over time for the emergence of the accommodation of differing value patterns. There is a need to mediate the public world of art, literature and school, with which the teacher is familiar, with the private world of the learner who struggles with personal and social problems. Bryk (1996) in dealing with Catholic schools argues that schooling is to nurture in students the feelings, expressions and reflections that can help them approach their relations to all the world.

Beck (1998) commenting on Bernstein (1996) has focused attention on the imposition by central governments of modernistic models of school structures. The introduction of the local management of schools has demanded the development of management capabilities which hitherto had largely been left to the local authorities. The management of schools previously was confined, although not wholly, to the day-to-day administration and the provision for teaching and learning. In recent years the schools have become hugely structured organisations with deputy headteachers, senior teachers and subject co-ordinators whose roles interrelate to create webs of support and development for pupils and staff. These webs can provide the care of pupils both in the pastoral and academic sense. They can also provide for the teachers a framework for the sustaining of professional standards and growth. Bernstein (1996) has argued that the changes brought into schools by the encroaching structures have also brought with them different ways of work, different criteria for assessment and different relationship patterns.

The managerialism of the school expresses itself in development plans, target setting, measuring outcomes and value for money. For teachers this has meant an increase in pressure to meet management agendas and to implement programmes of change. In turn this has led to the emergence of new kinds of identity which the teachers must embrace. Perhaps inevitably there has been the need for increased training for teachers to meet the demands made upon them; ultimately trainability becomes the object of teacher professionalism. This suggests that the teachers' future identities are uncertain but the need for the further training of teachers rolls on. How does this view of the changing role of the teachers affect the pupils in their charge? The constant stress on performance by the teachers – backed up by SATS, GCSE, A-levels and league tables – with the greater definition of the standards or competencies they should exhibit must carry over to the pupils in terms of not only their daily performance in school but also in their expectations of how their adult lives will be moulded by influences outside themselves. This view seems to suggest that what is happening is much more complex than any simple notion of 'cultural imposition' might suggest. What is being witnessed is a far more far-reaching set of changes. It is the transformation of the institutional relationship through which we are governed and our lives are regulated. Cowen (below) reflects a similar view in tracing the changes in the place of the university in the education system and the growth of the cult of performativity. The measurement of success of a university is seen in the short term and based on levels of registration, throughput and graduation. It is also measured in the 'value' of research undertaken and the volume of output. More esoteric studies and analyses must take second place to higher profile academic and vocational studies, the value of which may be assessed by the potential it has to provide for future national growth in the materialistic sense.

Hargreaves (1994) counsels the desirability of accepting the challenge to redesign school structures to help teachers work together more effectively as a community in collaborative cultures of shared learning, positive risk and continuing improvement. This argument is combined with a view that more collaborative structures 'can create the necessary conditions for collective and continuous improvement. Such communities are difficult to establish and maintain in large organisations or under conditions of rapid change' (pp. 256–7).

Hargreaves goes further and calls for collaboration within schools as a process for restructuring, and for this process to be set within an ethical discourse and political parameters. The danger of over-decentralisation of change to the school level is the potential for chaos to ensue. Guidelines provided by central or local authorities would help individual institutions to identify their own potential for change. However, with Pring (below),

Hargreaves asserts such ethical principles are contestable and should be open to public debate to set nationally agreed goals and frameworks (though not specific and detailed contents) which guide the educational systems in which teachers work. 'From my own value standpoint, the principles of equity, excellence, justice, partnership, care for others and global awareness should be high in the agenda' (p. 259).

Each of the principles will permeate the school structures and affect the conduct of the school as well as the relationships within it. Care for others is a potent force for the development of a community which respects individuals and their diverse needs. A wider expression of concern for others comes through a broader spread of interest and investigation which is encompassed in global awareness. Gardner (below) argues strongly for a review of subject foci to explore the possibilities for replacing the parochialism of much that is taught to encourage a firmer understanding of the world, its peoples and the richness of our cultural heritages. Hargreaves reminds us of Zeichner's (1991) conclusion:

> Although we need to encourage and support a process of democratic deliberation within schools that includes parents and students as well as administrators and teachers, we need some way of making determination about the 'goodness' of the choices that emerge from these deliberations. (p. 368)

A language of deliberate reflection and evaluation is called for to test the worthwhileness of the conclusions of much deliberation. This apparent call for restriction upon freedom of choice may lead to challenges of undue control, but Beyer and Liston (1996) in examining the nature of freedom concluded that freedom of action does not provide guidance for the actual steps to be taken. Barber (1992) considered liberty not to be solely one of endless choice; people feel free when these choices are meaningful. This provides the framework for choices based on ethical or religious values chosen when 'they participate in the free communities that permit them to define common leads autonomously and establish common identities freely' (p. 25).

Cairns (below) reinforces the need to recognise that individuals live within a range of ecologies from which they draw their values and to which they also contribute their own perceptions. Each individual, child or adult, lives within a small community, probably the family, where acceptable patterns of behaviour in all its forms are practised. The same individuals also experience and interact in a wider community, perhaps the school or workplace, where potentially some different rules and values may apply. Further wider communities can be described and Cairns sees these widening communities as being nested one within the other and the individual being required to live, work and interact in all. Through these varying experiences the individual develops patterns of activity which are agreeable and acceptable to everyone. Those patterns may vary in detail and the individual has to adjust to the changing context of experience daily. The individual making adjustments has to be guided by a set of values which need to be flexible enough to withstand the adjustments and sustain the person. Without that flexibility and accommodation the individual could not survive in the fast-changing environments that are met daily. The same flexibility will sustain the individual throughout life in adjusting to changes that come over time.

Cairns argues that the curriculum must be fitted to the local community and the global context. The starting point should be the collective wisdom of the teachers and other educators, including parents, who will contribute to the curriculum development process. With Hargreaves (1994, p. 85), Cairns (below) acknowledges the context-dependent character of the knowledge base of teaching which respects the need for teachers to make judgements in their own schools and classrooms.

WHAT NEEDS TO BE DONE NEXT?

Whilst this chapter has placed emphasis on schools, it will be recalled that at the beginning the reader was reminded that all institutions express values through the organisation and conduct of programmes of studies. Universities that offer highly structured but rigid courses appear to stress the importance of a deep immersion into a particular field of study. Other universities which encourage a more flexible programme with greater opportunity for choice of modules within an overall degree structure place greater responsibility on the student to select packages which will provide a coherent focus for study. Other universities may offer an even more liberal selection of topics for study. Each pattern offers comment on the perceived capabilities of students and the faith placed in them to make appropriate choices.

In the post-compulsory sector of further education the breadth of courses available offers considerable scope for choice by the student in the qualifications to be achieved. The organisation of the timetables and the flexibility of choice offered may go a long way to give messages to the students of the worth that college administrations place on both subjects and qualifications. The ethos of the college may be reflected in the opportunities for study offered, the length of courses, and the potential combination of subjects which underpin the structure of the timetable developed. Colleges which give greater prominence to academic as opposed to vocational studies provide firm and unequivocal messages about the worth of courses.

Schools which make decisions on their organisation and the allocation of resources based on competencies may offer to the pupils messages which are clear in their support for academic or professional success. Schools which place a greater stress on other areas of the curriculum, such as art, music and drama, provide clear signposts of the worth attached to the affective development of pupils. These are real-life decisions in every school, for, although the national curriculum provides a structure which ensures some degree of uniformity between and across schools, there is at the same time ample opportunity for schools to allocate resources to support the perceived targets of the school. Cairns (below) argues that we should seek to find the purpose, identity and process of values education through an exploration of the territories in which an institution – school, college, or university – enters in order to engage all its members in 'the development of values as a life-long process and not something that is completed by early adulthood' (Raths, Harmin and Simon, 1978).

In summary, as Taylor (below) argues, we must continue to address the aims of education in values, the context for education in values, and conflicts in values and education in values. A language of valuing and of reasonableness will lead to institutions and individuals within them being sensitive to ways of valuing, and lead ultimately to ongoing reflective evaluation in action of all in whichever context they find themselves.

REFERENCES

Barber, B. R. (1992) *An Aristocracy of Everyone: The Politics of Education and the Future of America.* New York, Ballantine.

Beck, J. (1998) *Morality and Citizenship in Education.* London, Cassell.

Bernstein, B. (1996) *Pedagogy, Symbolic Control and Identity: Theory, Research and Critique.* London, Taylor & Francis.

Beyer, L. E. and Liston D. P. (1996) *Curriculum in Conflict: Social Visions, Educational Agendas and Progressive School Reform.* Tenham College Press. Teachers College, Columbia University.

Bryk, A. S. (1996) 'Lessons from Catholic High Schools in Renewing our Educational Institutions', in T. McLaughlin, J. O'Keeffe and B. O'Keeffe (eds), *The Contemporary Catholic School.* London, Falmer Press.

Bryk, A. S., Lee, V. A. and Holland, P. B. (1993) *Catholic Schools and the Common Good.* Cambridge, MA, Harvard University Press.

Giddens, A. (1990) *The Consequences of Modernity.* Cambridge, Polity Press.

Hargreaves, A. (1994) *Changing Teachers, Changing Times.* London, Cassell.

Lawton, D. (1996) *Beyond the National Curriculum: Teacher Professionalism and Empowerment.* London, Hodder & Stoughton.

Pring, R. (1995) *Closing the Gap: Liberal Education and Vocational Education.* London, Hodder & Stoughton.

Raths, L. E., Harmin, M. and Simon, S. B. (1978) *Values and Teaching.* 2nd edn, Columbus, OH, Merrill.

SCAA (1996) *The National Forum for Values in Education and the Community.* London, SCAA.

Senge, P. (1992) *The Fifth Discipline: The Art and Practice of the Learning Organisation.* London, Century Business.

TTA (1997) *Standards for the Award of Qualified Teachers Status.* London, TTA.

Ungoed-Thomas, J. (1997) *The Visions of a School: The Good School in the Good Society.* London, Cassell.

Zeichner, K. M. (1991) 'Contradictions and Tensions in the Professionalization of Teaching and the Democratization of Schools', *Teachers College Record*, 92(3), 363–79.

2

MORAL VALUES: THE CHALLENGE AND OPPORTUNITY

Archbishop of Canterbury, Dr George Carey

My predecessor of long ago, Archbishop William Temple, tells in one of his books that when a group of bishops in 1926 attempted to bring the government, coal-owners and miners together to end the coal strike, Mr Baldwin, then Prime Minister, asked how the bishops would like it if he referred the revision of the Athanasian Creed to the Iron and Steel Federation! It seemed self-evident to the Prime Minister that the task of the Church was to relate to things spiritual only and thereafter it was interfering. William Temple had little trouble showing that morality is indivisible. Whether we talk about social and economic order, the private world of the individual citizen, the task of teachers in their important responsibilities and, more topically, political vision, all these areas and more are proper concerns of the Church and church leaders.

I am grateful, then, to share some of my concerns for the moral formation of our children who are our joint responsibility. I do so out of great respect and admiration for the teaching profession. I am well aware that sometimes teachers have to take an unfair share of the blame for disappointing standards and delinquent behaviour. Certainly not enough regard has been paid to the tremendous commitment and successes of so many teachers.

'Moral Values: the Challenge and the Opportunity' was chosen to reflect on the initiative of the Schools Curriculum and Assessment Authority (SCAA) to see if the teaching profession with co-operation with its partners could arrive at an agreed basis of shared values to transmit to children. But I would like to begin my reflections not from within the classroom but from the larger vista of society. Lord Nolan (1996) remarked:

In our first Report we said that 'the great majority of men and women in British public life are honest and hard-working and observe high ethical standards'. Nothing I have heard in our subsequent studies would lead me to a different conclusion. The sheer numbers of people who believe that it is right for them to give something to public service – not just in the relatively high profile areas that my Committee investigates, but also in countless numbers of local charities or church groups – augurs well for the health of this country.

I believe that this is a good starting point because it is positive and constructive in two dimensions. It is a reminder that we do not need to base our interest in the moral and spiritual dimensions of education on some sort of indiscriminate despair about contemporary society. As Lord Nolan says, vigorous moral commitment is alive and well. We see it in the vast numbers who volunteer for public service. We see it in the extraordinary and humbling commitment of so many people to care for dependent relatives, even at the cost of many of their own dreams. We see it in the rising concern and reverence for the environment and for other parts of the animal kingdom and, despite loose generalisations about a secular society, we see it in the strong interest which many millions of people still show in organised religion and which many others show in other less institutionalised forms of spiritual exploration.

I emphasise, therefore, that I am not basing this chapter on a reactionary desire to return to some notional golden age in the past, nor on blindness to what I see as many encouraging signs of virtue and spiritual awareness in society today.

Lord Nolan's words are also a reminder that in some areas of life we have recently done better in thinking systematically about our moral beliefs and standards in order to encapsulate them in formal Codes. This conscious re-definition of expected ethical norms is a way of refreshing and re-owning such beliefs and transmitting them to our successors and descendants. The pessimist will say that the need for such written Codes is a sign of moral decay, but optimists like myself will see them as a positive step forward, an act of moral will which leaves less scope for ambiguity and laziness over non-negotiable ethical standards. The work of Lord Nolan's Committee is one example of this. Others include increasingly impressively elaborate Codes which are developed by, for example, the BBC in handling different aspects of its broadcasting responsibilities.

Nonetheless, we cannot take any of this for granted. This, indeed, is one of my key themes. Values and morals do not grow on trees or fall like manna from heaven, or just look after themselves. On the contrary, they are always vulnerable to the darker side of human nature, such as selfishness, greed, self-deception, vanity, lust and cowardice. Virtues need hard work, careful nurture and a continuous process of modelling, discussion, appropriation and internalisation across the generations. They require energetic commitment and activity. It is not something that just sorts itself out if only the individual is allowed maximum autonomy. That implies, to *my* mind, both a naive optimism about the capacities of unaided individuals and totally false assumptions of so-called 'autonomy'. In practice every person is subject to all kinds of external influences, for good or evil. It is, in fact, a cop-out if we pretend that people do not need a great deal of help in developing their capacity to make moral choices in life and to work out their own mature beliefs about what is good and right for themselves and for the society of which they are part. As the Chief Rabbi has put it, you cannot express yourself as a moral and spiritual person if you do not have a spiritual or moral language.

That brings me to the heart of what I want to say about 'Moral Values: The Challenge and the Opportunity' which confront us. Every person needs a moral language, and society needs a moral language, if it is to be a civilised, just and peaceful society at all. We cannot base our work together for the common good on reticence, embarrassment and incoherent mumbling, yet that is the state into which the discussion of morals and values has descended in many parts of Western society today. The main culprit is the popular cultural assumption that to try to define something as good and right in an absolute sense is an unwarranted and potentially oppressive incursion into a domain which should be purely private. What is right is simply what feels right for me. What is good is simply a matter of individual opinion and hence it is arrogant and disrespectful of other people's autonomy to tell them what is good. Morality is privatised; relativistic suspicion becomes the standard response to any talk about moral standards and it is found uncomfortable, even embarrassing, to discuss morality in public. As a result, God is also banished to the private domain as a hobby or private consumer choice, which suits some people just as bird-watching, eating Chinese takeaways or going to keep-fit classes suits others.

In fact, this beatification of individual autonomy is a chimera. I agree very strongly with the Chief Rabbi's argument in his recent excellent book *The Politics of Hope* (1997) that extreme libertarianism is as much the enemy of liberty as is authoritarianism and despotism. As the Chief Rabbi points out, the classic nineteenth-century champions of liberty like J. S. Mill understood very clearly that liberty requires and rests on moral values. Without values, such as trust, honesty, consideration for other people, love of justice and peace, there can be no liberty, because there can be no orderly society within which individuals can grow and express themselves in interdependence with others.

Let me put this more strongly; if the citizens of a country do not internalise respect for law and the responsibility to behave fairly and peacefully towards other people, there is no external power on earth which can secure peace and justice. We can go on expanding prisons and security forces endlessly with no impact on the crime and injustice into which society will descend. Relying on external agencies to police the values of civilisation simply will not work. It is up to us – every one of us, every single responsible person – to be accountable to one another.

I believe that most reasonable, thinking people will conclude that there are at least three things wrong with the assumption that what is moral is just a matter of individual opinion. Firstly, we can recognise instantly that it undermines the basis on which we seek together to work for the good of all. The idea of positively working for the common good goes straight out of the window. Secondly, it is not true; anyone who lives in a family knows that not for one day can we live simply for ourselves. Thirdly, nearly everybody actually knows it is not true. In my view, the vast majority of people, even if they articulate the cultural assumption that morality is a purely private affair, actually have strong beliefs about some things that are absolutely good and others that are absolutely evil.

'Ah!', comes the response, 'but those beliefs are just obvious values like not killing or hurting other people, doing as you would be done by and things like that!' If you look around our society, you will see these values are not so obvious or bland after all. And, in fact, the list of shared values is much more extensive than such a reaction implies, and this is a vitally important point. Let me take you to one source of shared values which has for generations shaped this nation – indeed, Western Europe. It is called the Ten Commandments. The first four commandments are about God – worshipping Him and valuing Him. As I shall explain in a moment, we shall not all agree about those and we shall not agree about the authority for the Ten Commandments. But the remaining six are very practical values – honouring your father and mother, you must not murder, you must not steal, you must not commit adultery, you must be truthful and you must not covet. These six social commands are relevant to life today, and will indeed receive widespread assent from many who do not describe themselves as religious. Indeed, they challenge an exaggerated and rather sloppy theory of 'pluralism' which holds that there are now so many different beliefs and philosophies and ethical choices around that we do not really have shared beliefs any more.

According to this view, we are, in effect, an atomised collection of individuals, each with his or her own particular beliefs and the role of the state should simply be to maximise the autonomy in which these atomised individuals can pursue their own choices and preferences. But this extreme interpretation of pluralism is in fact a gross distortion. It is a distortion in one dimension because it is statistically ridiculous to treat Christianity as just one among a jumble of competing and equal faiths in our society. It is a distortion in another dimension because many important shared beliefs bind us together despite our philosophical and religious differences. We must get out of the one-eyed approach of respecting differences but failing to recognise shared values and indeed all that flows from our common humanity.

Let me repeat the important distinction I made in relation to the Ten Commandments. We shall not all agree on one single source of authority which legitimises the values we hold in common. Many of us are theists, and others are not. Some would describe their beliefs about the meaning and purpose of life as religious, others as humanist (I for one am unwilling to allow the label 'humanist' to be purloined exclusively by those who do not believe in God – but that point is for another occasion). Perhaps I should add that among those who are practising Christians, for example, there are also some pretty important differences about the relative authority to be assigned to the Bible, the tradition of the Church and the prayerful discernment and experience of the individual. These differences about the authority for doctrinal and moral teaching do of course lead to differing opinions on particular ethical issues within, as well as between, different Christian denominations. When we then broaden the cast of characters to include all those of other faiths and none, we are obviously not going to agree on the authority or sources of our beliefs, but that is a fundamentally different proposition from the argument that we have no shared values any more. It is perfectly possible and normal to have different views on authority and different views on particular ethical questions and yet to have strong shared values which we can nurture and build on together for the good of all.

Nor do I accept that shared values, simply because they may be supported by a number of different religious and philosophical systems of belief, must therefore somehow be anaemic and bland. On the contrary, people with different religious and non-religious beliefs can in my experience work together for all they hold in common with faith, hope and love. The shared values of society deserve to be debated and defended with passion as well as reason. And there is a vast inherited store of parables, poems, drama and wise sayings from Christian and other traditions which can fill apparently bland concepts with life-enriching significance and emotion.

If all that I have said forms part of the moral vision of a mature and civilised society, where do schools, churches, home life and the wider community fit in? We all fit in as part of the moral matrix through which individuals are formed or, conversely, 'de-formed' as civilised and caring people. Allow me to use the phrase 'moral companions' of the role we should play. I am aware that it is commonplace to use the term 'mentor' but that smacks uncomfortably too much like the idea that 'we have all the answers' instead of sending the proper message that each one of us is on a journey of moral growth and development and that it is only with the greatest of humility that we can show others a better way. If we wish to model attractive lifestyles for children, then we can never assume that we have arrived at a state of perfection. Moral companionship thus speaks of a shared journey with our children, learning from their insights as much as they from ours.

I must emphasise again, as I did when I introduced the subject in the debate in the House of Lords on 5 July 1996, that it would be wrong to burden schools with unrealistic expectations as to what they can achieve by themselves. Already, in general, schools are very moral places by comparison with most aspects of the society outside the school gate. Children spend far more of their time out of school than in it and if too many of the wrong messages and signals are bombarding children in their homes, in the streets and clubs and in front of TV sets, it is no good relying on schools alone to counteract all those other tendencies. While all these points may be gladly conceded, however, children spend a great deal of time at school during vital formative years, and it is of the utmost importance that, despite the difficulties, teachers should feel encouraged and authorised to transmit the shared values of society to children and promote these values deliberately and positively.

I am well aware also that many teachers, like many clergymen, currently feel that apparently endless extra demands are being heaped upon them. They feel that too many changes have been made on top of one another, that they are criticised unfairly for problems which are not of their making and that in general they are under-valued and misunderstood. I know that, in this climate, heightened expectations of spiritual and moral dimensions of education are not necessarily going to be welcomed with huge enthusiasm by the profession at the very same time as they are being expected to raise standards of numeracy and literacy and help their schools compete more successfully in the league tables of examination results.

I do understand all this, but as with beleaguered and misunderstood clergy, policemen, social workers, farmers and many others, an unduly negative or defensive posture tends to make matters worse rather than better. It would be wrong to say: 'Well, because of all the pressures on them arising from the league tables, we had better ease off on the moral and spiritual side of education.' On the contrary, it is precisely because there are many pressures to make education more utilitarian – a better bargain for UK plc – that all of us, including teachers, need to insist on a balanced and rounded concept of education as set out in the 1988 Education Act. We want people who leave school to be good citizens and good neighbours, not just stuffed heads and effective contributors to the economy. We want them to be people who are competent in exploring and appreciating the spiritual side of life, and what it is all for, as well as competent at computer programming, mathematics and foreign languages.

Moreover, although the conspicuous success of many Church schools in the recent league tables should be interpreted with caution, and should certainly not be crowed over, there is surely a clear indication that having a strong ethos and a sturdy framework of shared values running through the whole school life may be a means of producing good examination results.

I gladly accept and affirm the corollary that if as a society we wish to raise, rather than lower, the expectations we have of schools, there are clear implications for the status and respect and support which we give to schoolteachers. Especially when we take the moral and spiritual dimensions of education into account, as we must, we need our schoolteachers to be substantial, respected figures who can be expected to carry authority and conviction as they seek to help pupils develop their moral and spiritual capabilities along with other competencies.

One of Benjamin Franklin's favourite quotations was this: 'The noblest question in the world is "What good can we do in it?"' Summarising much of what I have stated thus far, I believe that a great deal of education at school and beyond should centre on that question.

In that context, and against the background of damaging tendencies to extreme moral relativism, I indicated strong support in my speech to the House of Lords in July 1996 for the initiative of the Schools Curriculum and Assessment Authority (SCAA) in convening a National Forum on Values in Education and the Community. When SCAA published the draft recommendations of the Forum, I, along with the other Presidents of the Council for Christians and Jews, reaffirmed my strong support for the search for non-negotiable shared values which could be imparted to children without reservation. We applauded the progress already made, whilst acknowledging the scope for significant strengthening in particular areas. I understand that, much to the surprise of some of those attending the Forum, an impressive and sturdy consensus emerged about a whole series of values, thus exploding the myth that we do not have shared values any more. I do not agree that these values are bland or obvious or uninteresting, although like any words they need illustration and dramatisation and human modelling in order to bring them to life. It is a succinct Report, but almost every line in it is capable of elaborate and exciting embodiment in different aspects of the curriculum and the ethos and rules of the school community. The values are grouped in four categories as applying principally to the healthy functioning of society, our relationships with other people, our understanding and development of ourselves as individuals and our approach to the environment and future generations.

It is important to be clear about what the Report of the Forum claims to be, and what it does not claim to be. It seeks to describe what the shared values of a wide cross-section of society *are*. That is a different question from what they *should be*. As a Christian leader, for example, there are plenty of additional Christian teachings which I would want to add and which no doubt Church schools will add.

Let me point out that such additions are not necessarily negative. Christianity is not primarily a moralistic religion. That is not to say that morals are unimportant; it is not to say that Christians are indifferent to moral standards, of course not. What people find puzzling to grasp is that Christianity is not first and foremost about following moral rules as much as following a master and teacher who leads the way. The New Testament does not set out to be a rule book; it calls us to follow someone who makes sense of the human condition and who calls us to love God and love our neighbours as ourselves. Within that framework, I and my colleagues in the Churches will continue our work of trying to influence the consensus of society further in the direction of Christian teaching. Hence, the statement of values by the SCAA National Forum does not purport to be the Churches' statement of the ideal or indeed anybody else's statement of the ideal, but it does reflect some very important core values which bind us together, despite our differences, and to which we can all gladly assent. I am not somehow surrendering my integrity as a Christian leader by affirming and promoting the shared values of society as a basis on which all schools can build. Specifically Christian mission activity and the elaboration of a distinctively Christian doctrine are of fundamental importance to other dimensions of my ministry, but I can also gladly sit down with other people of all faiths and none and work together on the basis of shared values for the good of society. I am indeed delighted that this is the approach which SCAA has encouraged and brought to fruition as a first stage.

Few of us would want to deny that the influence of the home as paramount *in* moral development. There in the behaviour of parents and siblings are to be found some of the most important moral companions of impressionable and vulnerable young people. Families have the prime responsibility for transmitting the norms of civilised society to each new generation; and families, especially prospective parents and parents, often need a great deal more support in that task than they currently receive. Since the statement of values from the Forum covers many different areas of life, as I have explained, I am wary about treating any one subject as a symbolic totem as to whether the statement is 'sound' or not. I am, however, of course aware of controversy about the treatment of marriage, a topic which I certainly regard as of great moral importance along with many others. As I understand it, the document says that we should support families in raising children and caring for dependants; we should support the institution of marriage; and we should recognise that the love and commitment required for a secure and happy childhood can also be found in families of different kinds. I know there has been vigorous and proper debate about whether the wording should be stronger or whether additional points should be made. As I have explained, I and many others would no doubt want to make additional and stronger points if we were setting out our own full beliefs, but within that framework I have no difficulty in accepting the statement of the Forum as a consensus which exists now. To my mind the specific mention of support for the institution of marriage can be translated into a great deal of new thinking and classroom work about the institution of marriage, why it is important, what it needs in order to flourish and what people entering marriage need to think about. I believe that the time has come to stop arguing about particular words in the statement and to move on to the huge and vital task of considering what the implications of the words are for the curriculum and activities and ethos of the school. I want to emphasise that the development of a robust statement of such a considerable consensus on shared values is a major achievement and could strengthen the crucial partnership of schools and parents in their common task of nurturing the young people they have different but joint responsibilities for.

I am delighted that over the last few years there has emerged a growing concern about moral values. We have all begun to see that it makes practical sense. The social and personal damage done to us all when evil triumphs is plain to us all. Think of the social cost of dishonesty in the workplace; think of the social and personal cost of crime; think of the personal and socials costs as family relationships collapse. In a society disfigured by widespread moral confusion and false theories of privatised morality, a commitment to a shared set of values is a most significant prize. I noticed that a moral word entered the 1997 Election campaign: 'trust'. I welcome this word. We want politicians we can trust but it is not only politicians who have much to gain from being people who can be trusted. We all need to be so: Church leaders, media people, businessmen and business women, parents and teachers. But behind this beguiling and seemingly innocent word 'trust' lurks a morality directly associated with the challenge and opportunity that I have been addressing, because trust is dependent upon truthfulness, honesty and all the other virtues that are required for the revitalisation of a good and just society. As Barbara Misztal says in her book *Trust in Modern Societies* (1996): 'We are not social because we are moral; we are moral because we live together with others and therefore need periodically to account for who we are. Morality matters because we have reputations to protect, co-operative tasks to carry out, legacies to leave, others to love and careers to follow.'

Against this background, my message concerning schools and the curriculum is therefore this: 'Because we all want a just and moral society, let us affirm the Statement of the National Forum for what it is – not the ideal, but a statement of shared values as they are not, let us give strong backing to it as a starting point and let us get working hard on the next stage of translating the words into the reality of teaching and behaviour in schools themselves.' Many good things are already being done, and these should be affirmed and strengthened; in other areas, it may be necessary to develop the curriculum and supporting resource materials and training in order to do justice to the many different dimensions of morality encompassed in the SCAA document.

I congratulate all those involved in the SCAA initiative, I thank all those in the education system who are already doing so much to make schools moral and good places for our children to learn and develop themselves, and I look forward to exciting new developments in this field in the years ahead.

REFERENCES

Misztal, B. (1996) *Trust in Modern Societies*. Oxford, Polity.
Nolan, Lord (1996) *Committee on Standards in Public Life, Volume I*. London, HMSO.
Sacks, J. (1997) *The Politics of Hope*. London, Cape.

3

VALUES AND EDUCATION: A CURRICULUM FOR THE TWENTY-FIRST CENTURY

Denis Lawton

Curriculum studies have often been defined in very narrow terms, perhaps as an aspect of the psychology of learning or programme planning. In the Curriculum Studies Department (now an academic group of the Institute of Education, University of London) curriculum has always been defined very broadly – so much so that some might say it includes most of educational studies. We talk of curriculum as who teaches what to whom for what purpose, and who decides. Clearly values are involved in all of those aspects of curriculum. But here I want to extend the definition even further and look at the institutions in which education occurs – especially schools. I want to suggest that the culture of the school is an essential, but neglected, aspect of curriculum studies.

WHAT IS WRONG WITH THE SCHOOL AS AN INSTITUTION?

There are several different kinds of possible answers. Let me start with the historical. The school even as we know it now was largely a nineteenth-century invention, deriving from new social theories and practices which gave rise to a number of different kinds of institutions including workhouses, factories and prisons. Schools shared a number of their characteristics – including architecture.

Such institutions were developed to solve social and economic problems. What they had in common was the need for a large number of 'inmates' to be *controlled* by a smaller number of supervisors. In all cases there were two features in common: strict discipline and hard labour. And to make the task of the supervisors possible certain practices and rules became customary, for example, silence, strict control over time (marked by bells, sirens or hooters) and restrictions of space (sitting in rows or in prisons – Bentham's panopticon) and movement (such as marching in lock-step). Many rules were necessary for this form of organisation which tended to be bureaucratic – of an autocratic kind. In all cases, including schools, control was the dominant factor.

Workhouses have been abandoned; prisons are generally thought to have failed but continue to exist. Schools have changed a good deal and have proliferated throughout the world. But have they changed enough? Do they still have too many features in common with nineteenth-century factories, prisons and workhouses?

Let me now move away from the history to a brief glance at the sociological study of schools. There is a vast literature here from Willard Waller's (1932, reprinted in 1965) classic study *The Sociology of Teaching* to more recent theses on school ethos and the culture of schools. What they have in common is the emphasis on control. Teachers and headteachers, parents and politicians all seem obsessed with control. And with schools organised as they are, control is certainly essential. But why is it so dominant an issue?

Part of the answer is that schools are wracked with contradictory aims. For example, one aim of education is to liberate the child from the constraints of ignorance; but we compel children to go to school. Emancipation and compulsion are strange bedfellows. A further contradiction is that children are compelled to go to school, but if they misbehave they are excluded – deprived temporarily of the right of access to worthwhile educational experiences. The role of the teacher also has its contradictions: the teacher must dominate the classroom, but must also be a model of adult behaviour; the teacher must appear to like all the pupils (even those she/he dislikes), whilst preaching the virtues of honesty and sincerity. Waller referred to one terrible definition of the teacher as 'a man hired to tell lies to boys' (we must forgive the sexism of the 1930s). But this is taking us away from the major concern – the school as an institution. One of the oddities that sociologists have analysed is that schools as institutions have more rules than would seem to be necessary: regulations about length of hair, colour of socks, for example, as well as the observation of numerous ceremonies and rituals. The Public School model has made many contributions: the house system, uniforms, over-academic curricula, age grouping (where else are human beings so rigidly classified according to their age?), grading and selecting. It has also often been pointed out that some of the functions of schools are themselves contradictory: personal development conflicts with selection and allocation; emancipation conflicts with socialisation.

S. B. Sarason (1990) was so concerned with these problems of school culture that he called one of his books *The Predictable Failure of School Reform*. The main thrust of the book concerns the inability of reformers to accept that past efforts at change have failed. This inability to diagnose past failures dooms their reforms to failure. The gap between rhetoric and reality is too great. Sarason quotes John Goodlad (1984) who made the point that schools are amazingly similar in terms of classroom organisation, atmosphere or ethos. School systems tend to be adversarial. The systems are very strong and resistant to change. Schools are very complex systems – to change them you have to get to know the culture. It is no use seeing unconnected parts.

WHAT IS CULTURE OF THE SCHOOL?

That brings us back to the idea of school culture. Many writers on school effectiveness and school improvement agree that school culture is the key element in the success or failure of change programmes. But they are often less than clear about what they mean by school culture. The term school culture must refer to the beliefs, values and behaviour of the teachers; one index of success will be the extent to which the school culture is shared by the pupils and supported by their parents. In many there is a gap between pupils and teachers; in some a counter-culture. Why?

A weakness of many studies is that they often take school culture as straightforward and simple, rather than attempting to submit the school to some kind of cultural analysis. The difficulty is that culture is essentially holistic, yet we need to find sub-categories of some kind if we are to do more than indulge in bland generalisations. Other writers have commented on the complexity of schools as organisations: seeing the work of schools as multi-dimensional.

One of the shortcomings of many studies which refer to the culture of the school, is that they use such terms as beliefs, values, attitudes, expectations, etc. as if they all exist at the same level of consciousness. There is a clear overlap between aspects of school culture and the need to change curricula. I have elsewhere (Lawton, 1996) suggested that it may sometimes be useful to analyse school culture at three different levels: behaviour (including the visible aspects of curriculum, pedagogy and assessment) being part of the surface culture (or ethos); fundamental beliefs being part of the deep structure of culture; with attitudes and values existing somewhere in between the surface culture and the deep culture, but overlapping both of them.

A school's vision might be determined by deep-rooted beliefs, but there may be contradictions at all levels – for example, there might be a commitment to social justice and equality of opportunity in a comprehensive school, but conflicting with those principles would be deep-rooted assumptions (beliefs) about intelligence, ability and social class which would influence teachers' behaviour in the classroom. To make pedagogical changes would require a willingness to get to grips with those cultural contradictions. This is not easy. Similarly, a school might have a surface commitment to equal opportunities for boys and girls, whilst individual members of staff might retain assumptions about what girls could or should do.

David Hargreaves (1995) has suggested that one aspect of school planning would be to reach an appropriate balance between the expressive (social cohesion) and the instrumental (social control). Hargreaves has encouraged the move away from over-simple models by using a two-dimensional (or two-domain) approach to school culture – using the terminology of 'instrumental' and 'expressive', previously employed in a different context by Bales (1951) whose interest was in how the tension between the two was resolved. Hargreaves extended the two concepts to the study of schools. 'Instrumental' is about task-achievement, and for Hargreaves, social control; the 'expressive' function is concerned with social cohesion – maintaining good social relations.

Both the dimensions are expressed as high, optimum and low, avoiding the usual assumption that high is better (see Table 3.1)

TABLE 3.1

Instrumental domain (social control)

		High	Optimum	Low
Expressive domain	High	C		B
(social cohesion)	Optimum		E	
	Low	A		D

The model generates four ideal types A, B, C and D with a fifth E – a different concept of the effective school.

Type	Characteristics
A Formal	High pressure to achieve learning goals (including exams), and perhaps games; but weak social cohesion between staff and students. School life is orderly, scheduled, disciplined. No time wasted; homework regularly set and marked; tests frequent; prizes; expectations high; low toleration for those who do not live up to them.
B Welfarist	Relaxed, carefree, cosy atmosphere; informal friendly teacher–student relations. Individual student development within a nurturing environment; child-centred and democratic; work pressure is low; academic goals are easily neglected in favour of social cohesion goals; truancy and delinquency low.
C Hothouse	All under pressure to participate; high expectations for work and personal development; teachers enthusiastic and committed; everyone seems to be under surveillance and control; high anxiety; reduced independence, autonomy and individuality. A 'total institution' (Goffman, 1968).
D Survivalist	Social control and cohesion weak. School close to breakdown. Social relations poor; teachers striving for basic control, allowing pupils to avoid work in exchange for not engaging in misconduct. Lessons leisurely. Teachers feel 'on their own'. Many pupils alienated and bored; delinquency and truancy high (as is staff absenteeism).
E Effective	The ideal school of the effectiveness literature. Expectations of work and conduct are high; school is demanding but enjoyable.

Hargreaves makes a further interesting point: some of the great classical sociologists (Comte and Durkheim) were concerned with the problem of *under*-regulation (or loss of traditional forms of control), while others (Marx, and in a different way, Rousseau) were concerned with *over*-regulation. One sociological perspective is to see a tension between 'alienation' (Marx) and 'anomie' (Durkheim).

I suggest that many schools are too concerned with control for the historical and sociological reasons briefly described above. What we need to do is to re-think the functions of the school in the twenty-first century, with the intention of changing the organisation of schools so that pupils take more responsibility for their own learning. Not a programme of total individualised self-instruction (because social learning is also very important) but a considerable shift in the balance away from teacher direction to individual responsibility and ownership of the teaching–learning process.

VALUES: WHAT IS WRONG WITH THE CULTURE OF THE SCHOOL?

Desirable Changes in the Cultures of Some Schools. I suggest the following:

1 Less bureaucratic and hierarchical organisations – flatter structures.
2 Changes in power relations – principals, teachers, students.
3 The school should be a learning community (more like college/university).
4 Broader views of learning/intelligence.
5 Better balance between group learning and individual progression.
6 More flexible and dynamic pedagogy.
7 Professional development of teachers.
8 Taking account of stressed and over-burdened teachers.
9 The need to recruit and retain good-quality teachers.
10 School development planning should involve all teachers.

WHAT IS WRONG WITH THE CURRICULUM?

The national curriculum is based on a series of false assumptions:

1 That it is possible to plan a curriculum for today and tomorrow by looking backwards to what schools have always done. Bruner (1960) mentioned this tendency in terms of driving with too much emphasis on the rear-view mirror.
2 More specifically, it is assumed that a curriculum should be planned by listing ten or eleven subjects and then specifying detailed content.
3 That planning by objectives is the best way.
4 That in all subjects the most important aspect is memorisation of content.

5 That cognitive development is more important than the social, moral and aesthetic development of pupils.

6 That assessing pupils' achievement on the curriculum can be used to grade teachers and their schools (assessment as social control).

7 That assessment by external tests is better than teacher assessment (more control).

The result in the Education Reform Act 1988 was a missed opportunity to plan a curriculum for the 1990s and into the twenty-first century. In 1988 teachers were presented with a national curriculum which, although extremely detailed and time consuming, still did not cover all the necessary aspects of life indicated in a preamble to the national curriculum: political, economic, social and moral development.

To counter the criticism that the national curriculum was inadequate because many important aspects of development and experience were not covered by the Foundation Subjects, the National Curriculum Council produced 'NCC Circular No.6: The National Curriculum and Whole Curriculum Planning' (NCC, November 1989). It recommended that every school should plan its whole curriculum bearing in mind cross-curricular dimensions, themes and skills. This document was followed by more specific suggestions. For example, 'Curriculum Guidance 8: Education for Citizenship' (NCC, 1990) offered 'guidance on ways in which education for citizenship might be strengthened and ensured in every school'. The other four cross-curricular themes were economic understanding, health education, careers and the environment: each had its own NCC guidelines. This initiative might have gone some way to correct the limitations of the ten-subject approach. But the NCC advice was a non-starter for two reasons: first, it was non-statutory – competing for time against the over-specific, compulsory national curriculum; and, second, some Education Secretaries, especially Kenneth Clarke, were hostile to what they saw as unnecessary complications, and discouraged the NCC from developing these cross-curricular elements. In any case, the national curriculum ran into a variety of problems and in 1993 Sir Ron Dearing had to be called in.

Given that schools already complain that the timetable is over-crowded, how could all this additional knowledge be accommodated? The answer lies in the fact that the national curriculum has been (despite the Dearing Review, 1993) specified in far too much detail, on the assumption that much information needs to be covered and memorised. I am not suggesting that all memorisation is unnecessary, far from it. But it is clear that the whole question of what needs to be memorised should be reconsidered, not least in the light of easy access to computer-based encyclopaedias and other data.

I would like to recommend a massive reorganisation of the curriculum, not just tinkering at the edges. I have five major proposals.

1 From content and objectives to skills and processes

The Higginson Report (DES, 1988) complained that A-level students spent too much time memorising and recalling facts and arguments rather than acquiring fundamental understanding of the knowledge. Similar comments have been made about the curriculum for younger pupils. Robert Reich in *The Work of Nations: Preparing Ourselves for 21st Century Capitalism* (1993) has discussed the need for much higher levels of thinking skills in the computerised world of symbolic analysts. Bruner (1960) talked about process, structure and the need for children who were learning science to begin to think like scientists. The Cognitive Acceleration through Science Education (CASE) project at King's College, London has been very successful in improving learning in science for children aged 11–13. The aims of the project were broader than making science teaching more effective. It was concerned with the development of reasoning. The general assumption is that children develop their ability to think when they try to solve intellectual problems. Unfortunately in many schools teachers and pupils enter into an unconscious contract to avoid too much effort: teachers devise ways of keeping children busy on work that will not involve too much mental exertion. The aim of the CASE project was to raise expectations and standards. CASE lessons encouraged discussion and critical appraisal of tentative ideas. Teachers are urged to encourage the learners to reflect on their own thinking processes: 'How did you solve that problem?' 'Explain it...' Another key word is bridging. Thinking skills do not automatically transfer to different situations – connections must be consciously made. Teachers and learners develop certain kinds of 'high-level thinking', for example, control of variables, probability, correlational reasoning. The researchers conclude that the way to raise academic standards is not investment in content-based technology, but on well-targeted programmes to improve intellectual ability or thinking scientifically. They recommended focusing on the 11–13 age group. The Economic and Social Research Council (ESRC) has invested in wider application of similar methods in other subjects, such as mathematics and history. The 'Innovation and Change in Education' programme coordinated by Professor Martin Hughes, Exeter (see Hughes, 1993 and 1996).

2 From subjects and cognitive attainment to cross-curricular themes and the affective domain

Subjects may be useful up to a point, but they are limited – some of our most pressing problems are not conveniently packaged within a single subject. In real life we have to get beyond the subjects. The ten-subject national curriculum encourages concentration on traditional cognitive learning, but young people grow up unable to cope with real-life problems involving an understanding of their own society, including its political structure, and unable to cope with questions of values and morality. A dramatic shift in the direction of social and moral education may be our most urgent need.

Recent work in psychology has also shown that conventional intelligence tests have concentrated on one very limited form of ability and encouraged teachers to ignore many other kinds of intelligent behaviour. In the USA Howard Gardner's (1983) theory of seven kinds of intelligence reinforces the view that we should think of a broader curriculum. The traditional grammar school curriculum was too academic and neglected personal and moral development. The Gardner theory suggests that not only is the traditional curriculum too narrow in terms of human abilities, but also that we should be looking for abilities and talents in all pupils. Professional teachers will have a richer concept of 'ability', and will try to adapt teaching to the intelligences of the learners; children do not all learn in the same way, and, whilst it is not possible for all teaching to be individualised, it is possible for teachers to diagnose individual difficulties and take account of them. There is promising work in Canada and more recently in England (the Avon 'Learning to Learn' project).

3 From didactic teaching to self-directed learning

The National Commission on Education (NCE) Report (1993) drew attention to the need for older pupils to take responsibility for their own learning programmes. This does not mean that teachers should not continue to give direction (including some whole class teaching) but the emphasis should move, as students mature, in the direction of learning how to learn – learning how to become autonomous learners. Multiple intelligence theorising is related to the idea of self-directed learning. One of the greatest difficulties is for the teacher to encourage the whole class to move along in the same direction, whilst recognising that the styles of learning and the range of achievement will be considerable.

Part of the task for the teacher is to plan carefully what kind of learning needs to be individual, what should be learned in a group, and when it would be better to have a whole class presentation by the teacher, always bearing in mind that pupils benefit from verbal interaction with the teacher. This is a very different picture from children simply engaging in 'activities' either as individuals or in groups. One of the hostile stereotypes of the 'progressive' classroom is that teachers never teach the class as a whole, but set work for groups or individuals, or simply leave them to 'discover'.

There is a further complication: part of the teacher's plan should be to cater for different levels of ability. This is very difficult, and Neville Bennett (1987) has observed that: 'Approximately 40% of tasks matched pupils' capabilities but there was a strong trend towards the over-estimation of low attaining pupils and the under-estimation of high attainers.' This is a finding supported by HMI evidence (DES 1978, 1983 and 1985).

One of the most sterile arguments in the last 20 years has been the debate about the advantages and disadvantages of setting and streaming by ability. This debate misses the point: it is not enough to have a class set for ability – what is needed is a much more complex pattern of organisation and pedagogy to cater for a range of individual differences. In 1993 the National Commission on Education (NCE) recognised this and devoted a whole chapter in its Report to 'Innovation in Learning'. It was particularly impressed by 'flexible learning', where pupils learn to take some responsibility for their own learning programmes.

The National Commission Report also recommended that by the age of about 14, pupils should be equipped to work independently in a *flexible learning* environment. It goes without saying that the flexible curriculum demands flexible assessment: it is also necessary to avoid age-related testing.

4 From academic or vocational to integration of both aspects of experience

We need to overcome the false and sterile opposition of academic and vocational (see Richard Pring, 1995). Many outside education have complained about this characteristic of educational thinking. This is by no means an English phenomenon, but we have the problem intensified because our social structure is so dominated by class. Curricula should be designed with a view to eliminating the distinction between academic and vocational: young people need aspects of both traditions, as suggested by the IPPR (1990), the National Commission on Education (1993) and

Richardson *et al.* (1995) *Learning for the Future.* We need a curriculum which gets beyond thinking in academic and vocational terms: this will not be easy because the two concepts are deeply embedded, and segregated, in our culture. All pupils need more social and moral education.

5 From a national curriculum 5–16 to life-long learning

We have at last reached the stage where most young people stay on in education beyond 16, but although much lip service is paid to the idea of life-long learning, very little thought has been given to relating the national curriculum 5–16, or education 14–19, to providing related opportunities throughout the whole of working life and beyond. This is important not only because most people will need to change jobs four or five times, but because they need to have opportunities to continue learning actively for the rest of their lives. These opportunities need to be planned – they are too important to be left to the market.

CONCLUSION

We face the twenty-first century with two major unsolved problems in our schools: first, the culture and organisation of schools; second, the curriculum. Both problems are still dominated by nineteenth-century thinking about education. Politicians and others still tend to think of a school where young people have to be made to work: control of students by teachers now themselves controlled by late twentieth-century centralism is the order of the day. Then there is a curriculum which is out of date and simply does not meet the needs of young people growing up in a rapidly changing democratic open society. They are both aspects of the same problem.

REFERENCES

Bales, R.F. (1951) *Interaction Process Analysis.* Cambridge, MA, Addison-Wesley.
Bennett, N. (1987) 'Changing Perspectives on Teaching Learning Processes', *Oxford Review of Education,* 13(1).
Bruner, J. (1960) *The Process of Education.* Cambridge, MA, Harvard University Press.
Dearing, Sir R. (1993), 'The National Curriculum and Its Assessment: Interim Report', July, London, School Curriculum and Assessment Authority.
Dearing, Sir R. (1993) 'The National Curriculum and Its Assessment: Final Report', December, London, School Curriculum and Assessment Authority.

Department of Education and Science (1978) *Primary Education in England. A Survey by HMI* London, HMSO.

Department of Education and Science (1983) *Teaching Quality*. London, HMSO.

Department of Education and Science (1985) *Better Schools*. London, HMSO.

Department of Education and Science (1988) *Advancing A Levels* (Higginson Report). Report of a Committee appointed by the Secretary of State for Education and Science and the Secretary of State for Wales. London, HMSO.

Gardner, H. (1983) *Frames of Mind*. London, Fontana.

Goffman E. (1968) *Asylums: Essays on the Social Situation of Mental Patients and Inmates*. Harmondsworth, Penguin Books.

Goodlad, J. (1984) *A Place Called School: Prospects for the Future*. New York, McGraw-Hill.

Hargreaves, D. (1995) 'School Culture, School Effectiveness and School Improvement', in P.M. Creemers and D. Reynolds. *School Effectiveness and School Improvement: An International Journal of Research Policy and Practice*, 6 (1, March), Lisse, The Netherlands, Swets & Zeitlinger, pp.23–46.

Hughes, M. (1993) *Flexible Learning Evidence Examined*. Stafford, Network Educational Press.

Hughes, M. (1996) *Teaching and Learning in Changing Times*. Oxford, Blackwell.

Institute for Public Policy Research (IPPR)(1990), Education and Training Paper No.1 'A British "Baccalaureat": Ending the Division Between Education and Training' (D. Finegold *et al.*). London, IPPR.

Lawton, D. (1996) *Beyond the National Curriculum: Teacher Professionalism and Empowerment*. London, Hodder & Stoughton.

National Commission on Education (1993), *Learning to Succeed*. London, Heinemann.

National Curriculum Council (NCC) (1989), *Circular No. 6: The National Curriculum and Whole Curriculum Planning*. York, NCC.

National Curriculum Council (NCC) (1990) *Curriculum Guidance 8: Education for Citizenship*. York, NCC.

Pring, R. (1995) *Closing the Gap: Liberal Education and Vocational Preparation*. London, Hodder & Stoughton.

Reich, R. (1993) *The Work of Nations: Preparing Ourselves for 21st Century Capitalism*. London, Simon & Schuster.

Richardson, W. *et al.* (November 1995) 'Learning for the Future', Initial Report London, Institute of Education University of London Post-16 Education Centre and the University of Warwick Centre for Education and Industry.

Sarason, S.B. (1990) *The Predictable Failure of School Reform: Can We Change Course Before Its too Late?* San Francisco, Jossey-Bass.

Waller, W. (1932 reprinted in 1965) *The Sociology of Teaching*. New York, Science Editions, John Wiley & Sons.

Part II:

The Context for Education in Values in Schools

The Complete Poems of Emily Dickinson

4

THE CULTURAL CONTEXT OF EDUCATION IN VALUES

Marianne Talbot and Nick Tate

In January 1996 the School Curriculum and Assessment Authority held a conference 'Preparation for Adult Life', the aim of which was to discuss schools' promotion of pupils' spiritual, moral, social and cultural development, and, in particular, to discuss values education and the difficulties schools face in providing it.

There were 200 delegates, many of whom submitted papers. It was their view, although most schools were managing to promote pupils' spiritual, moral, social and cultural development, despite the other pressures on them, this was becoming increasingly difficult and they would welcome guidance. The main difficulties, delegates decided, were that people lack confidence in the teaching of values because, believing that in a pluralist society such as our own there are no common values, they worry about *whose* values to teach and because they sometimes feel unsupported by society in this vital task.

Accordingly the conference recommended that SCAA set up the National Forum for Values in Education and the Community and give it a two-fold remit:

1 To decide whether there are any values that are agreed on in society.
2 To decide how best society might support schools in their promotion of pupils' spiritual, moral, social and cultural development.

The National Forum for Values in Education and the Community was set up in the spring and met over the summer of 1996. It consisted of 150 people drawn from across society, divided into groups of 15, all but one of which met three times.[1] It became clear very quickly to Forum members that there were values that they agreed on and on which they believed the rest of society would agree. A statement of these values was drafted (not without difficulty) and SCAA asked MORI to find out whether others would agree with the values outlined.

MORI sent the statement of values to 3,200 schools and to 700 organisations with a membership representative of the population at large, as well as doing an omnibus poll of 1,500 adults. In each case the result was similar – approximately 95 per cent of those who responded to the questionnaire were prepared to agree to the values outlined. This is a striking consensus and it provides excellent evidence for the claim that there are common values, despite the pluralist nature of our society. It also suggests that society has a duty to support schools in the teaching of these values, because pupils who do not understand them or act in accordance with them are likely to be out of step with the society in which they live.

On the basis of this the Forum recommended that the statement of values be used, by schools locally and by SCAA nationally, to:

- instill confidence (and in particular to provide an answer – our values – to the question 'whose values should we teach?')
- trigger debate (because agreement on values is wholly consistent with disagreement on the ordering, the application, the sources and the interpretation of these values)
- elicit support, from society generally and the local community in particular, for schools' work in this area.

The Forum also recommended that SCAA produce guidance for schools on their promotion of pupils' spiritual, moral, social and cultural development, using the values outlined in their statement as a starting point. These recommendations were accepted by Authority members in February 1997 and by the Secretary of State in May of that year.

This is the background to the work that SCAA's successor, the Qualifications and Curriculum Authority (QCA), has been doing on schools' promotion of pupils' spiritual, moral, social and cultural development. In the rest of this chapter we shall say more about this work whilst locating it in its cultural context.

THE CULTURAL CONTEXT OF VALUES EDUCATION

To locate values education in its cultural context is to clarify its meaning and/or purpose by considering it in relation to society and its customs, and to the activities that pertain to the cultivation of the mind. This chapter aims to develop a better understanding of values education by describing the way in which it: (a) relates to our society, (b) is embedded in education more generally, and (c) relates to a school's local community.

THE SOCIAL CONTEXT

Three major social changes – the secularisation of society, the fluidity of modern lifestyles and the development of the idea of a 'global village' – have had an enormous impact on the way in which we think about values over the last 40 years. In this section we intend to outline the nature of these changes, and their impact on the way in which we, as a society, think of values and discuss the consequences of this for values education.[2]

Traditionally God has been the authority to which people have appealed in defence of the reality of the difference between right and wrong, and in defence of the authority of moral rules. One of the difficulties generated by the increasingly secular nature of our society, therefore, is the question of the reality of the difference between right and wrong, and of the nature of moral authority. If God does not exist, then is the difference between right and wrong simply a matter of social custom, pragmatism or personal choice? If God does not exist, do moral rules have any authority? And, if they do, from where do they get it? From social custom? Pragmatic considerations? Or personal decisions about lifestyle? Anything and everything, it seems, becomes possible once God is deleted from the picture.

The secularisation of society has resulted in the widespread rejection of the major religions' teachings on divorce, living together and sexual activity outside marriage. This has ensured that more and more children are living in non-traditional households and/or experiencing family break-up, both of which present major challenges to traditional values as people strive to find their own way without tradition or custom to guide them.

The fluidity of modern lifestyles also loosens the ties of tradition and custom, dissolving the notion of community and exacerbating, thereby, the dearth of guidance on how life should be lived. Once the extended family, life-long friends and colleagues, who expected to spend a working lifetime together, could be relied upon to provide guidance (sometimes unwanted and usually implicit) on how life should be lived. Such a network of people, whose concern for each other and approval or disapproval of, and interest in, each others' actions, could have a significant effect on daily life. Now many peoples' lives are much more self-sufficient, with families geographically dispersed in such a way as to prevent daily involvement, and friends and work-mates being often a function only of a certain life-stage, location or job and at a remove from each other's daily life.[3] Decisions about how life ought to be lived, and about what matters and why, have become more and more the province of the individual who may, or may not, choose to discuss them with, or be influenced by, those around them.

Finally, advances in travel and communications technology, have helped to generate the idea that the world is a global village, peopled by human beings whose differences can be recognised and celebrated as adding to the glorious mix. We are fascinated by different lifestyles, different customs and different traditions. Not only are they intrinsically interesting to us, they also provide us with models of ways of living other than those provided by our parents, friends or workmates. And given the pressures on us to make our own decisions about how life should be lived and our unwillingness to accept our own traditions and customs as our only guide, these alternatives become even more interesting: they enable us (more or less realistically) to try them out for size, as it were, in our own lives.

These social changes have, as might be expected, both good and bad consequences. Amongst the good consequences we would list the massive increase in individual freedom and self-determination, and the destruction of the sort of moral boundary that constituted a failure to recognise 'the other' as fully human and worthy of respect. Amongst the bad consequences we could list the tendency to believe that self-determination and individual freedom are all that matters, and the threatened destruction of all moral boundaries through the rise of a very unsophisticated form of moral relativism.

There can be few of us who have not shuddered as we read, for example, Jane Austen or Anthony Trollope, and think about the social constraints under which people, especially women, used to live. Although the scope for individual freedom and self-determination has fluctuated throughout history, there can have been few periods, if any, when the scope was as wide as it is today. Whereas Aristotle argued that human beings get their identity, their self-hood, from being embedded in a community, from their relations to others, we tend to think that human beings get their identity from their individual choices and actions, that their communities and their relationships are a bolt-on, an important bolt-on, but a bolt-on nevertheless. We can, if we choose, turn our backs on our communities, reject everything we have come from, slough off our responsibilities if they are interfering with our sense of who we are or who we would like to be. We can even feel somewhat guilty, repressed perhaps, if we are not giving full expression to our own desires and urges.

This has led to a great deal of flourishing of potential that would, under earlier conditions, have been wasted. The possibility of self-determination has enabled people to realise dreams, ambitions and abilities that might, in a different era, have gone unfulfilled and/or unexpressed. But it is equally indubitable that this freedom is not an unmixed blessing. Freedom can be frightening: the possibility of choosing brings with it the possibility of making bad choices; the fear of bad choices can bring with it a fear of making choices – a desire to leave every door open and to refuse to make a commitment to anything. Such a refusal itself amounts to a choice, and not always a good one. Fear of bad choices can also lead to the undermining of commitments made: after all, if the choice seems to have been bad, why not undo the commitment, start again, make a different choice in the hope that the next one will prove more satisfactory?

Perhaps in the final analysis, the pendulum has swung too far and we need to recognise that individual freedom and self-determination are not the only, or even the primary goal, but just one type of good amongst others. These others might include, for example, the sort of relationship that only true commitment can underwrite, the sort of society that can survive only if everyone is prepared to put the common good above self-interest, and the sense of personal achievement that can be derived only from having exercised self-discipline in living up to one's ideals, rather than having given into temptation.

Like the increase in individual freedom and self-determination, the erasing of some moral boundaries has brought with it enormous good. It was not so very long ago that differences of race, religion, class, gender and age and the rest were seen as boundaries beyond which the normal moral rules did not apply. (One, of course, should not lie to other gentlemen, but the ladies ... well ... One can beat the natives with impunity, but one's English servant cannot properly be treated thus.) Today's moral boundaries, however, are much wider, wide enough indeed to embrace every human being irrespective of race, religion, ethnic group, class, gender or age. We now – rightly – think it positively wrong to locate the moral boundaries along the lines that used to mark them, so wrong we are even prepared to impose legal sanctions on those who continue to locate them along such lines.

This has got to be a good thing – our common humanity makes these differences utterly irrelevant when it comes to according to every human being the respect they deserve. We now see our world as a global village because we see ourselves as just one type of human being amongst many other types of human being, each equally worthy of respect, each with a worthwhile story to tell and each as capable, potentially at least, of making decisions about right and wrong as every other.

But again, in our opinion, the celebration of differences has gone too far. There are differences, we believe, that should be condemned, that cannot and should not be treated simply as interesting variations in human beliefs and/or customs. We think, for example, that those who believe that it is morally acceptable to execute writers for speaking their minds, those who believe that female children or foetuses are of less value than male children or foetuses, and those who think it a perfectly proper pastime to mug elderly ladies, are wrong, morally wrong, and that this needs to be said loudly and clearly.

The difficulty is, we think, that the very proper humility that leads us always to consider the possibility that we may be wrong about something, especially something to do with how one should live one's life and what is right and wrong, can wrongly lead us to think that we go too far if we claim to be right. But this leads us straight into a rather unsophisticated relativism, not just about morality, but about everything else too. After all, if we can't say you're wrong, that what you believe contradicts what we believe, then we must either say *we're* wrong, or we must accept that we are right *and* you are right, relative of course, to our own worldview (or whatever). But this path leads us quite quickly to the belief that no one is ever wrong – not only nonsensical (because it is human nature to be wrong a lot of the time), but also abhorrent when it comes to certain moral views.

The time has come, we think, to recognise that, whilst we should continue to recognise and celebrate those differences that are irrelevant to our common humanity, those differences that simply add to the glorious variety of humankind, there are differences that threaten to *undermine* our common humanity, differences that constitute evidence for error. To the extent that we believe every human being should be respected, for example, we are duty bound to condemn the beliefs of those who think otherwise.[4]

In the social context we have described, values education needs to have two aspects. We need to encourage and support children in their attempts to become independent individuals capable of making the decisions they will have to make about how they should live their lives, but we also need to help them to understand, embrace and live up to, the values of their society, to understand that it is not the case that anything goes and that there are goals other than individual freedom and self-determination.[5]

We are not alone in thinking that the time has come to halt the pendulum (whilst strenuously resisting any temptation to let it swing back too far in the other direction). Everywhere around us we see signs of people being worried about the direction in which our society seems to be headed, signs of people wanting to reassert the importance of the difference between right and wrong, the importance of responsibilities as well as rights and the importance of the common good as well as individual freedom, the importance, generally, of our *values.*

Response to the work of the Forum has also suggested strongly that people are ready for a change and that they are prepared actually to do something about it. The debate on values has started and is spreading. The Institute of Directors has launched the Hub Initiative, designed to encourage better perceptions of business by encouraging business to identify and live up to its values, and is about to start the 'National Forum for Values in *Business* and the Community', modelled on SCAA's forum. The media too is examining its values, as are the armed forces, the voluntary sector and the police.

It seems to us to be perfectly appropriate that, as we look back to the millennium, people should be taking some time for reflection, some time to ask where we are going and why, and whether we are going the right way about it. This can only be helpful to schools because the more support they get from society the better. QCA is working with as many people as possible to ensure that those who are reflecting on values are also aware of the excellent work that schools do in promoting values amongst young people, helping them to be trustworthy, reliable employees, citizens prepared to work for the common good, loyal and kind friends and responsible partners, spouses, parents and stewards of the environment.

THE EDUCATIONAL CONTEXT

Since 1988 there has been a strong emphasis, in education, on the academic development of pupils. During these years the national curriculum has been implemented, league tables and national tests have been introduced, and there has been a great deal of activity to raise standards generally. This is a good thing. It would not be good, however, for all the reasons given above, if it were to lead to a neglect of pupils' spiritual, moral, social and cultural development. It was concern that this might be the case that led to the setting up of the conference that gave birth to the National Forum.

The response of the educational establishment to the work of the

National Forum has been extremely positive. It has been welcomed as evidence that we, as a society, have not forgotten what education is all about, evidence that we are aware of the fact that education must be *inspirational* as well as instrumental, and as evidence that we do, as a society, care for each child as an individual, rather than simply as exam or employment fodder.

It is undeniably the case that the current national curriculum does not put enough stress on values and on their importance to education. There is a great deal about the 'what' and the 'how' of education, but very little about the *'why'*. In the review of the national curriculum currently taking place, however, we have an opportunity to remedy this.

This new emphasis on values, however, is not simply a new emphasis on the successful promotion of certain values to pupils, it is also importantly an emphasis on the values *of* education in our society. And this seems to us to be vital because we cannot, as a society, expect our schools successfully to teach values to their pupils, unless we have sorted out what exactly we, in education, do value.

That people do value pupils' spiritual, moral, social and cultural development is clear from a recent consultative exercise undertaken by QCA in order to inform its advice to the Secretary of State about the review of the national curriculum (QCA, 1998). This consultation provides us with further evidence for the belief that we are not alone in thinking that values are increasingly coming into focus in the thinking of our society.

The consultation was intended to determine views, especially the views of those in education, on the values, aims and priorities of the school curriculum. To this end QCA commissioned a comparative analysis of the curriculum and assessment framework of 16 countries; an analysis of research findings and relevant literature; and a widespread consultation based on a questionnaire, sent to all schools in England, all LEAS, teacher, subject and specialist associations and further and higher education establishments, and on a series of focus groups of parents, governors, employers and pupils.

The findings of the consultation include evidence of a very strong consensus across the educational profession about: (a) the need for a curriculum that articulates aims and priorities in terms of fundamental values and (b) the importance of the promotion of pupils' spiritual, moral, social and cultural development as an integral part of a curriculum that supports the growth of the individual as a learner and the creation of a caring and just society. These findings will help to shape the review of the curriculum, with a view to ensuring that it properly reflects our educational priorities.

Still further evidence for a shift in focus towards values comes from the government's setting up of a number of advisory groups and task forces to look into this aspect of education. These include groups looking at Personal, Social and Health Education, Citizenship Education and Creativity and Culture. All this activity underwrites a real commitment to give some serious thought to these aspects of education, in the belief that it can be made (in its own way) as rigorous as, and with as high a status as, the more academic aspects.

Recommendations from all these groups, together with the information from QCA's pilot study of the guidance on pupils' spiritual, moral, social and cultural development, have fed into a special group set up within QCA to receive them (The Preparation for Adult Life group). It is the task of this overview group to ensure that all this information and these conclusions shape recommendations for work in this area that are both internally coherent and integral to the rest of the curriculum.

Of course there are those who are concerned that such an emphasis on values will undermine the work being done to improve standards in literacy and numeracy. This seems to us to be a mistake: there is nothing inconsistent about combining attempts to improve standards and attempts to improve our thinking about values and the way in which we promote values. Indeed they seem to us to be highly complementary. Children, after all, will not give of their best if they believe themselves as being treated by their school as a cipher. If children believe they are valued by their schools as individuals, as persons capable of taking responsibility, of making sensible moral decisions, as capable of appreciating the fruits of human creativity, they are much more likely to be motivated to work hard. Similarly teachers who believe that the work they do is valued for its own sake as well as for its success in producing exam results are more likely to be motivated to give of their best. The successful promotion, in schools, of sound values is an intrinsic good, but we believe it is also instrumentally good – it produces results.

The educational world is, we believe, a seedbed ready prepared for society's current concern about values, because it is itself concerned about values and geared up to do something about them. Again this is all to the good.

THE LOCAL CONTEXT

Just as we cannot expect schools successfully to promote values unless we as a society value the work that they do in this area and recognise its importance in our national life, so schools cannot expect successfully to promote values to their pupils unless they have made explicit these values and committed themselves to living up to them as far as they are able. Children and young people are excellent hypocrisy detectors and a school that claims to respect every individual but then fails to match its actions to its words will soon find that its pupils take no notice of its words. It is vital that schools take care to ensure that the values they teach pupils are those that inform every aspect of their own behaviour.

The more help and support that schools can get from parents and the community the better. It does not matter how well a school promotes values to its pupils if, the minute they leave the school gates, pupils see that these values do not inform the behaviour of those in the community. The active involvement of parents and the community, when it is possible, is a vivid illustration to pupils of the importance of the values that they are being encouraged to embrace. If these values are promoted consistently by their parents, their teachers and other school staff, and by those members of the local community they come across in their daily lives, children will start themselves to embrace those values.

Partly for this reason, QCA's guidance on the promotion of pupils' spiritual, moral, social and cultural development recommends a six-step process to a whole school approach to work in this area, the first step of which recommends that schools involve every part of the school community in this work. The six steps are as follows:

1 Identify, together with the school's immediate and extended communities, the school's values and its beliefs about the goals and purposes of work in this area.

2 In the light of the values identified above, decide on objectives for each Key Stage.

3 Review current school practice (looking at subject area, the extra curriculum and the school context) to:

   • identify current success

   • opportunities for further work.

4 Plan and implement the desirable changes.

5 Monitor and review progress.

6 Recognise and reward effort and achievement in this area.

The first step is vital because it is during this step that schools will identify their goals, what *matters* to them, the parents and to the community. The result of the first step will be an explicit statement of the school's values, a statement that is 'owned' by the school, the parents and the community, that is couched in their own language and that reflects the concerns based on knowledge of local conditions.

There are many schools which already consult parents and others in the community on their values. Many of them take the opportunity presented by new parents' evenings to consult parents, some hold special evenings or Saturdays on which they bring in parents, business partners and members of the local community to discuss the sorts of thing they believe the school should teach children about what it is to be a human being.[6] These schools report that the sense of community generated by such events, and the support they feel they can call on as a result, is palpable.

The other five steps of the process are designed to ensure that once the school's values are identified and made explicit, the result is not simply a mission statement that, although nicely illustrated, is put up on the wall and forgotten. If schools are to promote these values successfully it is necessary for them to 'walk their talk', to ensure that their actions, in every aspect of the school match the fine words on the mission statement.

The same sense of community can be generated *within* the school by a discussion of values. In our experience teachers are often surprised to discover that energy spent discussing why their subject matters (why it is *valuable)* is amply rewarded in increased energy as they remember exactly why they chose to teach their subject and what it is about their subject that they believe to be important. A vivid understanding of this is a marvellous motivator, and it generates just the sort of enthusiasm that underpins good teaching. Such discussions also serve to draw teachers' attention to the values they naturally teach in teaching their subjects and in teaching generally. The involvement of support staff in the discussion of the school's values is another motivator – everyone has a contribution to make, and most people are delighted to be asked to make it.

Pupils can (and have) also been involved. Some schools have simulated the Forum's deliberations with pupils and have been pleased with the sophistication with which even quite young children discuss such issues and with the importance they attach to them. Older children have always been concerned about values as they try to acquire an understanding of themselves and make decisions about how they believe life should be lived. A school that harnesses this sort of interest and energy in the attempt to determine and live up to its own values will find that relationships between pupils and the school will be greatly enhanced.

The work of the National Forum for Values in Education and the

Community, in providing empirical evidence for the existence of common values, has shown that if individual schools do put an effort into eliciting the views of parents and the community, they will discover that these views, generally speaking, will support their own.[7] The very recognition of this is helpful. But if it is a first step to a conscious and explicit effort on the part of the whole community to *live* the values they have identified as their own, it can revolutionise the whole ethos of the school.

CONCLUSION

Rarely do so many cultural conditions combine in such a way to be so conducive to a particular change of emphasis. The social context predicts an increased emphasis on values as we, as a society and as individuals, struggle to decide how life ought to be lived in the light of such an extraordinary and unprecedented number of changes and the new millennium. The educational context predicts an increased emphasis on values as standards improve and we struggle to ensure that the necessary emphasis on academic development does not threaten the importance we place on pupils' spiritual, moral, social and cultural development. And taken together these two changes suggest that the time is right for individual schools to harness the support of their local community in the struggle to identify and live up to their own values.

We are very optimistic that values education will soon come into its own. This is not because schools do not already teach values but because, until recently, the teaching of values has been largely implicit and often unrecognised for what it is. The changes we describe above suggest that values education will soon be subjected to the same professional scrutiny that has led to improving standards elsewhere. We think this will revitalise education and, in the long run, society itself.

NOTES

1. The odd one out was the media group – members of which came only to observe and report on proceedings, rather than participate – an interesting subject, we believe, for another paper!
2. Many other social changes have contributed to the changes on which we focus. We have chosen these three as particularly notable. Other contributing factors would be the increase in the standard of living, an increasingly materialist outlook and increased leisure.
3. It is tempting sometimes to think that the popularity of soap operas is the result of

people's longing for a network of people, the minutiae of whose daily lives are known to one over a long enough span of time to generate genuine concern and moral involvement.

4. To condemn *these beliefs,* that is, not *those who hold them* – there are all sorts of reasons why people might hold abhorrent moral beliefs, not all of them the result of moral turpitude.

5. QCA's guidance on schools' promotion of pupils' spiritual, moral, social and cultural development, the guidance written on the recommendation of the 'National Forum for Values in Education and the Community', recommends just such an approach to values education. This guidance, piloted in 150 schools nationwide, offers advice on how successfully to achieve such an approach. This is supported by case studies of schools already doing excellent work in this area, by a directory of resources recommended as helpful by these schools and by materials illustrating many different ways in which schools might achieve and monitor success in this area.

6. Business partners are often happy to help with financial support once the aims of such an exercise are explained to them.

7. Schools sometimes worry that the values of the community, if sought, will prove to be at odds with those of the school. In our experience this is rare, and it is usually the result of a disagreement on the application of values that are shared rather than values themselves. The guidance discusses such cases.

REFERENCE

QCA (1998) 'Values, Aims and Priorities of the School Curriculum', Advisory Report of QCA Research, London, QCA.

5

SCHOOLS, COMMUNITY AND THE DEVELOPING VALUES OF YOUNG ADULTS: TOWARDS AN ECOLOGY OF EDUCATION IN VALUES

Jo Cairns

THE PERSONAL NATURE OF VALUES AND THE ALIENATING ENVIRONMENT OF A PLURALISTIC CULTURE

Schools have been charged since 1944 with the development of the physical, social, moral and cultural life of pupils and of society, without any agreement generated by society in general, government in particular or a school examination system of the model student(s) who should emerge from this process. In such a climate values education has proceeded more or less along the lines promoted by Raths, Harmin and Simon (1978):

> People have to prize for themselves, integrate choices into the pattern of their own lives. Information as such does not convey this quality of values. Values emerge from the flux of life itself. Consequently we are dealing with an area that is not a matter of proof or consensus but a matter of experience. (pp. 33–4)

They go on to warn:

> The development of values is a personal and life-long process. It is not something that is completed by early adulthood. We should be learning how to value. (p. 35)

For young people over the last 20 or more years the process of valuing and recognising personal values has taken place in a complex educational and social environment, roughly described as pluralistic. In a society in which a wide spectrum of values competes for attention and dominance, individuals, or their immediate social group, may feel uncertain and exposed. A situation of anomie may be described but possibly the more pervading situation is one of wholesale alienation.

The process of alienation for individuals and communities triggered by living within a pluralistic setting has a number of consequences. Those particularly which this chapter wishes to examine are:

- A seemingly endless quest for an identity: a phenomenon described so powerfully by Berger, Berger and Kellner (1973).
- The rootlessness caused by an unease of living at a time when confidence in the immediate past has been destroyed and there is no sign that a single homogenous new culture is even in embryo.
- The mapping of a territory as yet only partially discovered: what it means to be a developing person in a formal school setting.
- The place and contribution of a wealth of communities in the formal schooling of young people.

Underlying this examination will be a recurring insistence on asking the question: are formal schools the appropriate places to undertake the task of promoting the spiritual, moral, social and cultural development of young people as we look back on the millenium? To guide my responses to this question it is helpful to turn briefly to educators of earlier periods.

In the 1970s Richard DeLone writing in *The Saturday Review* spoke of:

> a society where institutions have generally failed the adolescent, a society in which family structure is in disarray, values are in confusion and the rites of passage from adolescence to adulthood are generally absent; a society ... in which adolescents have only an insignificant role and few places to go – except to a school. (DeLone, 1972)

THE ROLE OF THE SCHOOL IN VALUES EDUCATION AT THE PRESENT TIME

Formal education accounts for a noticeable portion of national expenditure and occupies the time and experience of young people for 35–40 hours per week for 11 years or more. If school is so invasive of young people's time, it follows that the experience must be recognisably cohesive for all concerned. In addition we are warned by George Counts

(1932) about the dangers of separating real-life experiences from the curriculum experiences by children in their schools:

> Place children in a world of their own and you take from them the most powerful incentives to growth and achievement. Perhaps one of the greatest tragedies of contemporary society lies in the fact that the child is becoming increasingly isolated from the serious activities of adults. (Counts, 1932, p. 5)

What are these pressing and overriding concerns of adults? The Tory government sought to define those concerns in relation to formal education in the White Paper (DfE, 1992) on 'Choice and Diversity'. These concerns would seem to be competition, choice and freedom, the very concerns which drive the current enterprise culture. At the same time the breakdown in personal and social values, exemplified most poignantly by the murder of James Bulger, within that enterprise culture caused the government to articulate the urgency of the promotion of social and spiritual values incorporated into the framework of the 1988 Education Reform Act through the establishment of a 'National Forum for Values in Education and the Community' by the School Curriculum and Assessment Authority. The present government in outlining a Third Way in Political and Economic thinking suggests that a climate will emerge in which values rooted in human and economic experience will be acquired through a common citizenship in a pluralist culture. However, the headteachers and school leaders, whose work it is to develop and implement the curriculum and social and moral relationships of the school (sometimes called ethos or culture), on which the dual aims of school experience are now focused, still tread uneasily.

Since the introduction of the Education Reform Act (1988), the government has handed the responsibility for planning and implementing their policies in the areas of the moral, spiritual, social and cultural development of their pupils and of society to the individual schools. Specific advice on these areas has been limited to a SCAA Discussion Paper, 'Spiritual and Moral Development', which was originally published in 1993 and republished in September 1995, and to the OFSTED, 'Framework for the Inspection of Schools'.

In the former, schools are reminded that moral development involves several elements:

- the will to behave morally as a point of principle
- knowledge of the codes and conventions of conduct agreed by society

- knowledge and understanding of the criteria put forward as a basis for making responsible judgements on moral issues
- the ability to make judgements on moral issues.

OFSTED inspects and evaluates schools' provision for spiritual and moral development and pupils' response to this provision ...(Their) discussions and observations should indicate whether the school for example:

- has an agreed approach to the ways in which spiritual and moral issues should be addressed throughout the school
- promotes an ethos which values imagination, inspiration, contemplation and a clear understanding of right and wrong
- offers opportunities in the curriculum for reflective and aesthetic experience and the discussion of questions about meaning and purpose
- makes adequate provision for Religious Education and collective worship.

The present situation thus teaches us that there is a crucial need for schools and particularly the leaders of schools to ensure that the teaching and learning of values is subsumed into the larger complex of activities in formal schooling.

Much of the debate about the nature of the educational experience currently provided in our schools highlights the tensions for systems charged with these tasks within current educational legislation. Articles by Richard Pring (1996) and Alan McClelland (1996) are particularly helpful in pointing to the difficulties in these areas. In the same collection, looking at the contemporary Catholic school, however, we find Bryk powerfully arguing that 'we live through our institutions' (Bryk, 1996). Headteachers', teachers', governors', students' lives are all effectively transformed as a result of their individual experience of their schools. How can we best ensure the transformation of the whole person as a result of their school experience.

A WAY FORWARD THROUGH THE SCHOOL–COMMUNITY CONNECTION

To meet the challenge of contemporary concerns for adults and young alike, values education might usefully consider the models of practice offered in the literature on 'school and community' relationships. We find there that it is valuable to examine the contexts in which schooling takes place in order to analyse the potential which schools as institutions have to respond to the challenge.

Schools themselves are complex institutions that serve varied and competing aims. Leo Rigsby in Reynolds and Wang (1995) outlines a fruitful method by which to reflect our schools. He argues that it is best to:

> see them as structures that are intimately and irrevocably woven into others, all of which serve political, economic, cultural, religious, and social aims. The interrelated nature of such institutions makes it almost impossible to plan and implement change in one without affecting the others. (p. 7)

This argument has lead to the need to contextualise or define the 'embeddedness' of each school. Thus Yancey (1995) and Saporito (1995) argue that their data indicate that the character of schools they examined in Chicago are affected by the complex social, economic and ecological processes beyond the population of the school and that these factors must be brought into play in any evaluation that addresses the crisis of (inner-city) education.

From his study of school–community connections in New Haven, Comer (1987) concluded that it is unwise to separate academic from social and emotional development in children, and that there is a pressing need to incorporate all the resources of the school (including parents and the community) *into a common blend of care and education.*

So far the literature acts as a useful reminder to educators that the nature, practice and outcomes of our work in schools are dependent upon a range of interrelated factors, personal, social, institutional and economic in nature. In many ways research based on the culture of the school (for example, the seminal studies of Bryk, Lee and Holland (1993) and Flynn (1993) on Catholic Schools) has very helpfully guided reflection and research into individual schools and their processes of values education. The nature(s) of the relationships between the headteacher, teachers, students and parents is generally explored as a dynamic one and the notion of 'culture to be constantly constructed and reconstructed by the school community' (Bates, 1986) is acknowledged.

Nevertheless, Lawton (1996) reminds us that the idea of school culture is used often with imprecise understanding of its meaning. He argues that for the word 'culture' to be used with meaning it must 'refer to the belief, values and behaviour of the teachers (including the headteacher)'.

Lawton's hierarchical plotting of 'beliefs,' 'attitudes and values' and 'behaviours' in the cultural map of a school will lead school managers and researchers into more subtle understanding, and evaluations of school culture as a whole. If we might use Lawton's own words to articulate the value of the model:

> Clearly this view of school culture will tend to emphasise many aspects of life, in addition to goals. Success or failure will not only be seen in terms of league table results. There is evidence that parents also look for much more than academic results when judging a school. It is very important that parents are encouraged to contribute to school life and planning in a variety of ways. (Lawton, 1996, p. 116)

TOWARDS AN ECOLOGY OF VALUES EDUCATION

It is more than 20 years since Eisner (1979) argued that the study of education needs a variety of new assumptions and methods that will help us appreciate the richness of educational practice. Eisner argued that 'the school culture functions as an organic entity that seeks stability, that reacts to changes in one part from changes in another's. We need to try to understand the interaction, if we seek intelligently to bring about significant change in schools' (p. 18).

Lawton's introduction of a further orientation in the cultural mapping of schools has indeed provided such a method. In what ways might such a map more radically direct the processes which contribute to the development of students who are able to be:

- participants in an economically productive society
- vocationally competitive
- competent to participate as citizens?

How might the schools contribute to the development of such individuals at a time when individuals and communities face:

- a seemingly endless quest for identity
- a sense of rootlessness
- the absence of an authoritative map of the territory to be covered for developing human beings at a time of cultural disjuncture?

Just as it is sometimes helpful to consider post-modernism as a complex map of late twentieth-century directions rather than a clear-cut aesthetic and philosophical ideology, so we might begin to consider education in values as a not yet clearly identifiable curricular or culture-based process. Rather we would seek its purpose, identity and processes through an exploration of all the ways in which a school engages all its members in 'the development of values as a life-long process and not something that is completed by early adulthood' (Raths, Harmin and Simon, 1978, p. 35).

Such a process is already underway. We might highlight the process by reference to the following:

1. The National Forum for Values in Education and the Community

The Forum was set up to take forward issues arising from the SCAA Conference *Education for Adult Life*. This conference took the view that, although society has the ultimate responsibility for the spiritual and moral development of young people, schools have an initial role to play and they would be better able to play this role if they could rely on a commonly agreed framework for values. The Forum was asked to make recommendations to SCAA on:

- ways in which schools might be supported in making their contribution to pupils' spiritual and moral development
- whether there is any agreement on the values, attitudes and behaviours that schools should promote on society's behalf.

2. Approaches to the teaching of citizenship

The work of the Citizenship Foundation has led to the trial and publication of curriculum materials to develop spiritual, moral and social values through a citizenship programme. The programme aims 'to contribute to the long-term development of confident, competent, morally aware citizens' (Rowe, 1996). The publication of the Crick Committee 'Report on Education for Citizenship and the Teaching of Democracy in Schools' and the awaited guidance for schools from QCA now provides the obligation and impetus for a renewed thrust in the curriculum towards the teaching of citizenship.

3. The promotion of the spiritual in education

Debate about the nature of the spiritual and its promotion in education has contributed to the tentative designs of a series of imaginative frameworks developed from a range of contributing disciplines, in particular psychology, philosophy and theology. The work of Alex Rodgers, Derek Webster and Andrew Wright in Best (1996) are particularly significant here (see also my own framework in Gordon, 1991).

The interplay of theological perspectives on spirituality, communal experience of spirituality and the experience and need for individual self-actualisation are particularly valuable. Perhaps we might point with Rodgers (1996) to Macquarrie's (1972) interpretation of spirituality to examine the place of spirituality within a wide range of human activities:

Fundamentally spirituality has to do with becoming a person in the fullest sense ... [and] ... this dynamic form can be described as a capacity for going out of oneself and beyond oneself ... It is this openness, freedom, creativity, this capacity for going beyond any given state in which he finds himself, which makes possible self-consciousness and self-criticism, understanding, responsibility, the pursuit of knowledge the sense of beauty, the quest of the good, the function of community, the outreach of love and whatever else belongs to the amazing richness of what we call the 'life of the spirit'. (pp. 40, 44)

4. The growth in studies of the educational values and systems of faith communities

The traditional areas of educational research, empirical, conceptual, evaluative and normative, are to be found in ever-increasing strength and complexity in the fields of Christian, Hindu, Jewish and Muslim education.

These four aspects of the process of engaging wide participation in mapping the life-long process of the development of values is remarkable in its extent and depth but not surprising. People and minority communities alienated by the fact of living in the domain of pluralist culture are beginning now to grasp the nettle of making their voice heard in the 'Naked Public Square'. This title suggests that the square is the place where public life is lived and the book argues that the place has been left naked, religiously and philosophically. The argument continues that among the mainstream churches the liberal concern to be fair to the pluralist society has created this nakedness. At the same time, the religious and moral vacuum has caused mainstream churches to lose their influence in public affairs and personal lifestyles. The book which is identified with discussion around the relationship between the individual and their community is *Habits of the Heart* (Bellah *et al.*, 1985), which argues that many Americans now recognise that they cannot sustain themselves by themselves when facing the complexities of contemporary life. They need some degree of connection in their lives if they are to find meaning and a sense of direction and control. There can thus be identified an intellectual, social, communal and personal awareness of the need (longing) for both involvement in the marking-out of the values which affect our public and social relationships and a public acknowledgment of such values.

Seemingly there is a momentum for a consensus on public values, which has grown out of an exhaustion partially brought about by liberal pluralism and by politicians' and religious leaders' current eagerness to chide and reprehend the general public for their lack of moral insight and direction. It is timely therefore to examine where such a route might lead. At the moment the momentum would seem to be swinging us away from the approach most widely advocated by John Rawls (1987).

Rawls commends 'the method of avoidance' in the face of pluralism in political life:

> we try, so far as we can, neither to assert nor to deny any religious, philosophical or moral views, or their associated philosophical accounts of truth and the status of values. (pp. 12–13)

Will the desire for guidance lead to imposed consensus? Or will the approach of the National Forum seeking 'any agreement on values, attitudes and behaviour' prove sufficient?

The experience of the British community over the past 25 years has been of a pluralism existing through the sheer fact of the presence side by side of a number of ethnic, religious and humanistic traditions, regulated principally by the Race Relations Act. To move from such a situation with its legal stimulus to public values to one of consensus as a means of developing and approving the values required to live and work together is at the very least disquieting.

The wider centralised community contains within itself a complex living map of possible directions. It is arguable that values education would benefit at present not from a hurriedly imposed national consensus, but rather from the opportunity to study the variety of human patterns or ecologies of values growth and discernment which so splendidly exist across our diverse pluralist community. In particular this would allow opportunities to arise to attempt to link the structure and organisation of the human valuing community with its localised environment. The questions asked of each ecology would surely lead to a public sensitivity and sensibility to the factors which allow for the flourishing of certain values and lifestyles in one environment. Only subsequently would the criteria emerge to evaluate whether such values and attitudes might flourish or not in a general and wider environment.

THE CENTRALISED ENVIRONMENT OF ECOLOGIES OF VALUES GROWTH AND DISCERNMENT: THE CIVIL SOCIETY

All ecologies in the UK exist within the context of a society still constitutionally tied to religion but more usually described, in line with other western states, as civil as opposed to repressive. Civil society is distinguished by its recognition of human rights as the basic rights of individuals. Religious freedom is specifically one of those human rights but this can be extended to religious communities themselves. It is a right to individual and community freedom. If religious freedom, as a basic right of individuals and of communities, belongs to the constituent principles of civil society, what consequences has this for the status of religion in such a civil society? In addition, civil society, as a secular temporal political order allowing different religions to operate alongside each other, goes further by declaring itself religiously and philosophically neutral.

Perceptions of the quality and opportunities of living in an increasingly recognisable civil society are now everywhere to be seen. Politicians, religious leaders, educators jostle for a public platform to voice their views. Sometimes the voice of the individual is listened to with particular seriousness and concern. For example, the perception and understanding of civil society raised by Frances Lawrence the wife of the murdered headteacher have been taken to heart at local and national level.

NESTED ECOLOGIES OF EDUCATION

The concept of an ecology of education enables us to explore that of an ecology of values growth and discernment, and opens up also the patterns of analysis and research necessary to a radical conception of the place of schools in the territory of values development and growth. The model of an ecology of values development and growth might make it possible to distinguish the salient characteristics of the social arrangements within which schools are embedded as a means of better understanding the outcomes of the overall educational process, which I have defined earlier as contributing to the development of students who are able to be:

- participants in an economically productive society
- vocationally competitive
- competent to participate as citizens.

A consequence of working with an ecology of education is the development of a central concept of 'nested' ecologies of education (see Bartelt 1995).

> As we examine macro-ecologies we unearth a second or third ecological system at work, much like the nested Russian doll. A classroom exists within a school and its ecology of teacher, classroom, physical structures and the like. Schools exist within a network of competing, complementary and other relationships as in cities, within a system of distribution of resources and constraints. Schools are only one part of the institutional ecology of cities and are affected by the neighbourhood ecology of the city. Finally cities are linked to each other in a complex ecology in which population, opportunities and fiscal capabilities are distributed differentially within the network. (pp. 161–2)

For our purposes the concept of nested ecologies illuminates our understanding that what takes place in schools is directly affected not only by the character of the communities from which the students are drawn but also by the macro-ecology of the civil society.

The wider society of course overlaps with the communities in which the school is based, with the teachers and students whose educational experiences are lived out in individual classrooms and across the wider culture of the school. Thus the concept of nested ecologies of education enables us to penetrate the layers of a school's culture better, to reveal those which are integral to specific school outcomes. For example, those aspects of education dedicated to cultural transmission are usefully sited in the nature and practice of relationships between the school and the local community, as well as the wider civil society.

In a case study of Mansfield School, Peshkin (1995), for example, examines the participation of the students in maintaining the local community. He concludes:

Most broadly considered, the school's social function addresses the well-being of society. A good citizen embodies the exigencies of this function for the benefit of all. (p. 244)

Peshkin then moves on helpfully to excavate the layers ('nests') of beneficiaries from the outcomes of the school's work:

- individual (students and their families)
- civic (the local, state and national community)
- professional (educators)
- ethnic (Italian, Mexican, Native American, etc.)
- doctrinal (including special interest and religious groups)
- occupational (electricians, accountants, secretaries, etc.)
- institutional (businesses and industry).

All beneficiaries can and do at some time claim to be stakeholders in the general business of education, as well as in the work and success or failure of individual schools. The combination of roles which any given number of stakeholders may fill at any one time, and its likely influence on the outcomes of the educational process, might again usefully be expanded through the 'nested ecologies' model. An example here might be taken from my own work for a project to bring about the professionalisation of a major aspect of a group of community schools. One person who worked closely with us proved to be a stakeholder as (i) a parent, (ii) committed religious adherent, (iii) major employer, and (iv) a significant private funder of communal educational projects.

ECOLOGIES OF COMMUNITIES AND VALUES EDUCATION

The complexity of the task implied in promoting the growth and acquisition of values in young people has underpinned the argument so far. At the same time, as we come to understand the significance of differences in cultures, in ethnic groups, in religious traditions, in the experience of women and men represented in our pluralist community, so we increasingly search for innovation in existing programmes of values education and citizenship. As personal confidence in articulating individual identities, community consciousness and increasing research output better informs us of the composition of our wider community so the need arises for a reappraisal not only of the programmes and form of delivery for values education adopted by schools but the settings in which such delivery takes place. Research findings are highlighting settings other than schools for the fostering of human development and nurture, such as the family, religious communities and specific forms of alternative formal education, such as the black supplementary school.

One way forward for schools to act upon such work would be to develop programmes which were customised towards particular groups or to open up whole-school programmes to change, with the inclusion of new role-models, diversity of cultural tradition in the expressive arts and literature, etc. Another way forward would be to examine the work of 'community schools' in values development and education. Pring (1984) reached the conclusion that:

> we need to attend in particular to the social and institutional setting which enhances or discourages these various lines of development … For Kohlberg, 'just communities' were a prerequisite for getting people to take seriously principles of justice in their daily behaviour. (p. 105)

The range of community schools covered might fall roughly under four headings:

- policoms – schools to serve groups of active citizens, cf Aristotle's *polis*
- relicoms – faith community schools
- ethnocoms – supplementary schools
- cultcoms – language and arts schools.

Such a step would be appropriate for the following reasons:

1 Communities are rooted either in localised environments or social and institutional networks of common concerns, interests and beliefs which affect young people at home in peer groups as well as at school (Bock, 1976; Cohen, 1974; Himmelfarb, 1977; Bryk, Lee and Holland, 1993).

2 A holistic approach to values education can be better achieved through emphasising the relationship between a person, or a group of people, and their immediate environment.

3 Community schools are provided in order to meet the established

needs of a group; programmes in education in values are tailored (sometimes through dialogue) to fit a specific group of young people. For example, summing up the day school phenomenon in Jewish life, Schiff (1992) quotes Ludwig Lewisohn, author, novelist and critic, who in his later years became a strong devotee of the day school movement. Lewisohn wrote in 1950:

The truest advance in recent Jewish history in the United States, the one altogether hopeful phenomenon, has been the initiation and slow gradual spread of the day school movement. It arose, necessarily, from classical Jewish sources ...

Fundamentals must be side by side with the acquisition of an exacting and elegant grasp of English and its literature. The usual [general] subjects of instruction must be augmented by Jewish history, symbol, ceremony, liturgy, with special attention in the grades to the development of the Yishuv, the community in Eretz Yisrael and the re-established commonwealth. All this can be accomplished in the [elementary] grade where a Jewish (day) high school is not practiced [sic]. The public grade schools take from six to seven years to teach so pitifully little that advanced educators see in these half-wasted years the chief symptom of the ills that afflict American education. They point authoritatively to the fact that in Europe boys and girls of seventeen to eighteen are ready for what we call graduate or professional studies.

Coming from such [day] schools Jewish children will be reasonably well educated for their age. The possession of one additional language, Hebrew, will make the acquisition of others in high school and college easier. Above all, these children will be, from the beginning, integrated Jews; that is to say, since they are Jews, integrated human beings. As such, as whole human beings, knowing their place in society and in the world, in the realms of man and God, they will be able to meet the non-Jewish world with ease, assurance, dignity. They will neither defensively overemphasize or fearfully underemphasize their Jewishness and their Judaism. They and they alone will be equals in temper, poise, directness of all social approaches of the Catholics and Protestants with whom they will have to mingle and compete in the daily involvement of American life.

Bryk (1996) speaks of Catholic schools in the following way:

In terms of the Catholic schools we studied, school life comprises a tradition of thought, rituals, mores and organizational practices that both invites students to reflect on this systematic body of thought and to immerse themselves in a communal life that seeks to live out its basic principles. The aim of this type of schooling is to nurture in students the feelings, experiences, and reflections that can help them apprehend their relations to all that is around them – both the material world and the social world, both those who have come before and those who will come after.

Isn't this what education should be about? Isn't this what we should want for all our children? At root here is a fundamental question: What in the post modern age is 'education for democracy?' The 'Catholic answer' involves a melding of the technical knowledge and skill to negotiate an increasingly complex secular world, with a moral vision which points this skill toward a more convivial and humane society, and a voice of conscience that encourages each student to critically pursue the vision. (p. 37)

4   Community schools are models of intergenerational activity focused on learning and human development within specific values and/or environmental frameworks. Community schools can foster the collaborative role of the family in the education of young people. They also highlight the very real issue of balance needed in securing the uniqueness of the individual family within the overall demands and goals of the community's educational needs.

5   The relational aspects of human and moral development are integral to community education; the corollary is that personal learning and growth are vital to participating fully in community.

6   It would permit a greater degree of understanding of the influences impinging on human development; a more sophisticated analysis of the degree of influence of individual parts on a young person's development might become available.

7   Community schools also must make decisions about the place of 'outsiders' or 'aliens' within their walls. A more compassionate response to the apparent alienation found in a pluralist culture might be forthcoming as each community tackles the issue.

8   The specific ethnic, religious, civic or cultural focus of the school is embedded within educational aims and activities. The integration of both within each student and teacher allows for the development of the reflective or 'examined life'. Each strand permits both a critical examination of the other as well as providing an integrating factor within the developing human being.

WORKING WITHIN THE MODEL OF ECOLOGIES OF COMMUNITIES AND EDUCATION IN VALUES

The paths of the student and the teacher within the teaching of education in values are not well signposted. We are aware of the negative impact however for individual development and mature growth in the wider community in which we live if the territory of values education is not even partially explored. Too easily stakeholders in the terrain seek to expose the shortcomings of all models advanced for values education.

Coming from a background in religious education which is so persistently attacked for its failure to deliver morally coherent and practising students to a wider community fractured by lack of belief and consensus, the discipline of beginning to work within this model has been particularly helpful. The overlapping worlds and roles in which the individual, the teacher, the family and their immediate communities move must all be seen to be playing their part in the growth and development of the individual and of values education.

AN ECOLOGY OF EDUCATION IN VALUES

To focus on the complexities of education in values within communities would seem a necessary part of the process involved in defining the ethics, practice and efficacy of values education in a plural community such as ours. First, the cultural, spiritual and moral capital embedded within those communities is part of the fabric of our present fragmented culture. It is essential that the communities are given the opportunity to share this capital.

At the very least the communities with a long tradition might be given the opportunity to understand themselves; at best they might speak to all about our present central human concerns with a message embedded in the social, moral, spiritual and cultural lives of our fellow citizens. Therefore in responding to and watching the ways communities conduct their (at least) public behaviour they provide all of us with:

> Extrinsic sources of information in terms of which human life can be patterned. Cultural patterns – religious, philosophical ... ideological – are 'programs'; they provide a template or blue print for the organisation of organic processes. (Geertz, 1964, p. 62)

Second, the work of defining and implementing school cultures within

our plural community which do not disable students in their valuing can
be best secured by access to a series of school cultures embedded in
specific local and social environments. Those many school cultures could
be open to evaluation on their suitability as modes of values education.

A provisional model for such an evaluation might take the following
shape through an examination of the following aspects of the school's
culture. Does the school culture facilitate:

- **A pursuit of 'practices'** which enhance personal and social
  well-being in so far as they are the source of shared meanings in
  life. Here the thinking of Alasdair MacIntyre (1990) in his work
  After Virtue is valuable:

By a 'practice' I am going to mean any coherent and complex form of
socially established co-operative human activity through which goods
internal to that form of activity are realized in the course of trying to
achieve those standards of excellence which are appropriate to and
particularly definitive of that form of activity, with the result that human
powers to achieve excellence and human conceptions of the ends and
goods involved, are systematically extended. Bricklaying is not a
practice; architecture is ... So are the enquiries of physics, chemistry, and
biology, and so is the work of the historian, and so are painting and music.
In the ancient and medieval world the creation and sustaining of human
communities of households, cities, nations is generally taken to be a
practice. (pp. 187–8)

- **Spiritual development** – The thinking of Macquarrie (1972) and
  Sutherland might be used as a basic here. Sutherland (1993)
  affirmed the 'fundamental need for a common language in which
  as citizens we can reflect upon the profound questions advanced
  by religion'. Sutherland recognised that, though there are
  powerful reasons for the attempt 'to make "non-sectarian"
  provision for the development of the spiritual', we have yet to
  reach a clear-cut agreed articulation of what that might mean. He
  suggests that we can pursue that clarification by developing
  Kant's remarks that 'the wonder and awe were induced in him by
  reflection upon "the moral law within" and "the starry heavens
  above"'; and concluded that this is shorthand for making central
  to education the task of self-understanding and the capacity to
  stare in awe and wonder at the world.

The very phrases 'self-understanding', 'moral conscience' and 'awe at the world' are redolent of the learner's engagement with a world that is to be lived in rather than merely understood; and understood for the sake of being able to live more fully within it.

- **Personal knowledge** – The school must start from where the learner is and find a shared language. Shared awareness of what is recognisably the sum experience can lead to the emergence of a language which communicates because it is understood from inside the experiences in which it is rooted. Here the work of Vygotsky (1978) and Polanyi (1964) are particularly helpful. The individual in such a school is thereby free to grow intellectually and make moral choices appropriate to himself and to his community in each generation.

- **Narrative** – The extent of debate about meaning not only to adopt shared meanings but also to adopt those which promise the accommodation of diversity within an overall unity of purpose. Here the work of Cupitt (1991) might illuminate the use made of literature (religious or otherwise) in the school for 'in the post-traditional age fiction is no longer rated as a poor second to fact as a mediator of "truths-to-live-by"'.

- **Embeddedness** within the local environment since emerging definitions of viable and ethical school cultures might involve continuous active involvement with the local community; comparisons may be made with existing attempts as in the work of Edgar Schein (1992). For Schein:

A pattern of shared basic assumptions that the group learned as it solved its problems of external adaptation and internal integration, that has worked well enough to be considered valid and, therefore, to be taught to new members as the correct way to perceive, think and feel in relation to those problems. (p. 12)

CONCLUSION

The process of valuing is lifelong. It follows that education towards it should be open-ended and recurring. As a life-long process it can include formal, non-formal and informal patterns. The non-formal and informal patterns of education traditionally lay great emphasis on the active participation of the learner in the decisions affecting his or her learning. It is only if the formal schools can unlock the individual from the belief that formal education is a time of incarceration in a system designed to lead to unrelated academic study that any form of education in values can occur.

Use of the Russian doll as analogy was made in the heart of this chapter. The smallest doll can only be found by searching through its larger models. Equally the tiny doll can only relate to its increasingly large companions by having the lid taken off the top. The concept of the doll would be incomplete without either the hunt through all the layers, taking each lid off to reach the tiniest doll or the scrabble to discover how the doll might be held together again. In our fragmented pluralist community the sources of life are not found in any one corner. As all living creatures seek out their place without an established map it is invaluable to look to other people in other corners and watch and wonder at how their commitments and values act as integrating foci for their communities. This chapter has attempted to argue there is much to be learned from our common enterprise of educating for growth in valuing. May I end with perspectives from two ecologies whose lives may have something to say about our common environment. William Lee Miller, in his review of the role of religion in American public life, has wondered whether the late twentieth century might not have been a time when the Catholic tradition's long commitment to the idea of human interdependence in community might not be just what is needed for the well-being of the American republic as it faces a complex and uncertain future. American culture has historically been orientated in a strongly individualistic direction by both its Protestant and Enlightenment sources. Miller observes that Catholicism possesses resources that both Protestantism and secular liberalism lack. These can help shape a response to both the challenges and opportunities of a world that needs a stronger sense of life being bound up with life, if it is to flourish in a way that befits the dignity of human beings. He calls this solidaristic vision 'personalist communitarianism':

> Something like such a personalist communitarianism is the necessary base for a true republic in the interdependent world of the third century of this nations's existence. And the Roman Catholic community is the most likely single source of it – the largest and intellectually and spiritually most potent institution that is the bearer of such ideas. (Miller, 1986, pp. 288–9)

In conclusion we would support this prescription to democracy offered by Clifford Longley (1995) in his introduction to Jonathan Sacks' book *Faith in the Future* as the basis for taking forward the role of community experience and wisdom in furthering education in values for our democracy:

> [It] requires an institutional habit of tolerance that goes beyond peace between factions, and deepens into an ability and willingness to listen and to learn. Faith communities will have their own clear principles, but may find that the uncompromising insistence upon those principles is possible only within their own ranks. They should not for that reason reject the effort to influence the community at large, nor should they give up if they are not totally successful. Faith communities serve the wider needs of society every time they offer moral principles that are out of step with the fashionable morality of the age, even when that offer seems not to have had any effect. In any event, *how can they know?* (pp. xiii–xiv)

REFERENCES

Bartelt, D. (1995) 'The Macrecology of Educational Outcomes', in L. Rigsby, M. Reynolds and M. Wang, *School-Community Connections: Exploring Issues for Research and Practice*. San Fransisco, Jossey-Bass.

Bates, R. (1986) *The Management of a Culture and Knowledge*. Melbourne, Deakin University Press.

Bellah, R., Madsen, R., and Sullivan, W.M., Swidler, A., Steven, M. and Tipton, S.M. (1985) *Habits of the Heart: Individualism and Commitment in American Life*. Berkeley, CA, University of California Press.

Berger, P.L., Berger, B. and Kellner, H. (1973) *The Homeless Mind*. New York, Random House.

Best, R. (1996) *Education, Spirituality and the Whole Child*: London, Cassell.

Bock, G.E. (1976) 'The Jewish Schooling of American Jews: A Study of Non-Cognitive Effects', unpublished Ph.D. thesis, Harvard University.

Bryk, A.S. (1996) 'Lessons from Catholic High Schools on Renewing our Educational Institutions', in T. McLaughlin, J. O'Keefe and B. O'Keefe (eds), *The Contemporary Catholic School*. London, Falmer Press.

Bryk, A.S., Lee, V.E. and Holland, P.B. (1993) *Catholic Schools and the Common Good*. Cambridge, MA, Harvard University Press.

Comer, J.P. (1987) 'New Haven's School-Community Connections', *Educational Leadership*, 44 (6), 13–16.

Cohen, S.M. (1974) 'The Impact of Jewish Education on Religious Identification and Practice', *Jewish Social Studies*, 36, July–October.

Counts, G.S. (1932) *Dare the School Build a New Social Order?* New York, New York Teachers College.

Cupitt, D. (1991) *What is a Story*. London, SCM Press.

DeLone, R. (1972) 'The Ups and Downs of Drug Abuse Education', *The Saturday Review*.

DfE (1992) 'Choice and Diversity: Autonomy and Accountability', DfE White Paper.

Eisner, E. (1979) *The Educational Imagination: On the Design and Evaluation of School Programs*. New York, Macmillan .

Flynn, M. (1993) *The Culture of Catholic Schools*. St Pauls, Homebush, NSW.

Himmelfarb, J. (1977) 'The Non-Linear Impact of Schooling: Comparing Different Types and Amounts of Jewish Education', *Sociology of Education*. 50 April.

Hollenbach, D. in McClelland, A. (1996) 'Wholeness, Faith and the Distinctiveness of the Catholic School', in T. McLaughlin, J. O'Keefe and B. O'Keeffe (eds), *The Contemporary Catholic School*. London, Falmer Press.

Geertz, C. (1964) 'Ideology as a Cultural System', in D. Apter (ed.), *Ideology and Discontent*. New York, Free Press.

Gordon, P. (ed.) (1991) *Teaching the Humanities*. London, Woburn Press.

Lawton, D. (1996) *Beyond the National Curriculum: Teacher Professionalism and Empowerment*. London, Hodder & Stoughton.

Lewisohn, L. (1950) *The American Jew, Character and Destiny*. New York, Frank Strauss.

Lieberman, A. and Miller, L. (1986) 'School Improvement: Themes and Variation', in S. Lieberman (ed.), *Rethinking School Improvement: Research, Craft and Concept*. New York, Teachers College Press..

Longley, C. (1995) 'Introduction', in J. Sacks, *Faith in the Future*. London, Darton, Longman and Todd.

MacIntyre, A. (1990) *After Virtue*. London, Duckworth.

McClelland, A. (1996) 'Wholeness, Faith and the Destructiveness of the Catholic School', in T. McLaughlin, J. O'Keefe and B. O'Keeffe (eds), *The Contemporary Catholic School*. London, Falmer Press.

Macquarrie, J. (1972) *Paths in Spirituality*. London, Harper & Row.

Miller, W. L. (1986) *The First Liberty: Religion and the American Republic*. New York, Alfred A. Knopf.

Peshkin, A. (1995) 'The Complex World of an Embedded Institution: Schools and Their Constituent Publics', in L. Rigsby, M. Reynolds and M. Wang (eds), *School-Community Connections: Exploring Issues for Research and Practice*. California, Jossey-Bass.

Polanyi, M. (1964) *Science, Faith and Society*. Chicago, Chicago University Press.

Pring, R. (1984) *Personal and Social Examination in the Curriculum: Concepts and Content*. London, Hodder & Stoughton.

Pring, R. (1996) 'Markets, Education and Catholic Schools', in T. McLaughlin, J. O'Keefe and B. O'Keeffe (eds), *The Contemporary Catholic School*. London, Falmer Press.

QCA (1998) *Education for Citizenship and the Teaching of Democracy in Schools: Advisory Group on Citizenship*. London, QCA.

Raths, L.E., Harmin, H. and Simon, S.B. (1978) *Values and Teaching*. Columbus, Ohio, Merrill.

Rawls, J. (1987) 'The Idea of an Overlapping Consensus', *Journal of Legal Studies*, 7, 12–13.

Rigsby, L.C., Reynolds, M.G. and Wang, M.C. (eds) (1995) *School-Community Connection: Exploring Issues for Research and Practice*. San Francisco, Jossey-Bass.

Rodger, A. (1996) 'Human Spirituality: Towards an Educational Rationale', in R. Best (ed.), *Education, Spirituality and the Whole Child*. London, Cassell.

Rowe, D. (1996) 'Developing Spiritual, Moral and Social Values through a Citizenship Programme for Primary Schools', in R. Best (ed.), *Education, Spirituality and the*

Whole Child. London, Cassell.

Schein, E. (1992) *Organisational Culture and Leadership.* San Francisco, Jossey-Bass.

Schiff, A. (1992) 'What We Know About ... The Jewish Day School', in S. Kelman (ed.), *What We Know about Jewish Education.* Los Angeles, Torah Aura.

Sutherland (1993) 'The Idea of a University', Lecture at the Conference on Universities in the 21st Century.

Vygotsky, (1978) *Mind in Society.* Cambridge MA, Harvard University Press.

Webster, I.H. (1996) 'Spiders and Eternity: Spirituality and the Curriculum', in R. Best (ed.), *Education, Spirituality and the Whole Child.* London, Cassell.

Wright, A. (1996) 'The Child in Relationship: Towards a Commercial Mode of Spirituality', in R. Best (ed.), *Education, Spirituality and the Whole Child.* London, Cassell.

Yancey, W.L. and Saporito, S.J. (1995) 'Ecological Embeddedness of Educational Processes and Outcomes', in L. Rigsby, M.G. Reynolds and M.C. Wang (eds), *School-Community Connection: Exploring Issues for Research and Practice.* San Francisco, Jossey-Bass.

6

THE CONTRIBUTION OF SCHOOLS TO PUPILS' SPIRITUAL, MORAL, SOCIAL AND CULTURAL DEVELOPMENT

Barbara Wintersgill

Every year HMCI publishes an annual report summarising the findings of inspections and the trends which have emerged in the previous 12 months. OFSTED also publishes papers on developments in the subjects of the national curriculum and religious education (RE). This chapter offers an overview of inspectors' judgements on the provision made by schools for the spiritual, moral, social and cultural development (SMSC) of pupils. The statistical data used here have been drawn from all inspections for 1997–98 and, where possible, comparisons have been made with 1996–97. Explanatory text is based on the examination of inspectors' reports and notes from a random sample of 30 primary and 30 secondary schools inspected during the period. All inspectors' judgements are graded on a seven-point scale where Grades 1–3 signify good or better, Grade 4 satisfactory and Grades 5–7 unsatisfactory or poor.

AN ANALYSIS OF THE PROVISION FOR SMSC

Table 6.1 draws a comparison between 1997 and 1998 for both primary and secondary schools. The table shows that in both primary and secondary schools there was very little variation between 1997 and 1998 in the percentages in each classification of grades, but that there were substantial differences between primary and secondary. For Grades 1–3 there was a difference of 10 per cent and in Grades 5–7 a difference of 7 per cent with the secondary schools making a substantially lower provision for SMSC. Primary schools are almost twice as successful in promoting moral and social development compared with spiritual and cultural development and they are more than twice as successful as secondary schools in promoting spiritual development. There is no conclusive evidence to suggest why spiritual development is so weak in secondary schools but the lack of collective worship in secondary schools *may* be a contributory factor. Other factors may include the teachers' lack of understanding of the nature of spiritual (and to some extent cultural) development. Interviews with teachers suggest that some are nervous of appearing to assume the supremacy of any single spiritual or cultural tradition, while others deny the value of introducing pupils to traditions other than their own. Figures 6.1 and 6.2 provide a basis for making comparison of the overall provision for SMSC at the primary and secondary levels.

TABLE 6.1:
COMPARISON OF GRADES BETWEEN PRIMARY AND SECONDARY SCHOOLS, 1997–98

Grades	Primary (%)		Secondary (%)	
	1997	1998	1997	1998
Good or better (1–3)	69	68	59	58
Satisfactory (4)	29	30	32	33
Unsatisfactory (5–7)	2	2	9	9

FIGURE 6.1
PROVISION FOR SPIRITUAL, MORAL, SOCIAL AND CULTURAL
DEVELOPMENT – PRIMARY

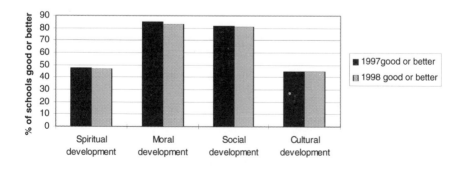

FIGURE 6.2
PROVISION FOR SPIRITUAL, MORAL, SOCIAL AND CULTURAL
DEVELOPMENT – SECONDARY

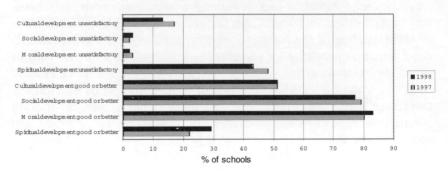

SMSC is not confined to one particular subject or area of study in the curriculum, although RE and collective worship do make important contributions. SMSC may be developed through all subjects, and the degree of contribution will depend upon the perception of the functions of the subject beyond the teaching of its basic material and upon the approaches adopted by the teachers and pupils. Figures 6.3 and 6.4 compare the unsatisfactory and good or better contributions of statutory subjects on the curriculum, and in general D&T, science, mathematics and IT have less impact than arts and humanities. This might have been anticipated given the nature of the subjects and the greater opportunities that humanities offers for the exploration of SMSC material.

FIGURE 6.3
CONTRIBUTION OF SUBJECTS TO SMSC – PRIMARY

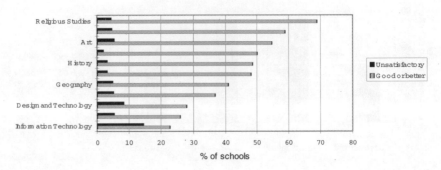

FIGURE 6.4
CONTRIBUTION OF SUBJECTS TO SMSC – SECONDARY

Contribution of subjects - secondary

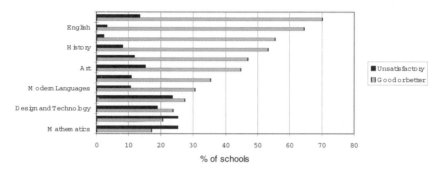

From this initial analysis it is possible to identify some of the characteristics of schools where SMSC is strong: where there is a clear statement in the school prospectus of the school's aims and, if appropriate, its religious principles; where the aims emphasise valuing and respect for people which permeate all areas of school life; and where a detailed and well-conceived policy is translated into practice by all staff. Where the school has a strong sense of community, where all the staff, pupils, governors, parents and members of the community work to promote school values and the learning ethos, and where this strength is reinforced by a supportive school culture, there is every expectation that the pupils will respect the values of the school as their own.

SPIRITUAL DEVELOPMENT

From Figures 6.5 and 6.6 it can be seen that the provision for spiritual development in primary and secondary schools is strongest in voluntary aided and voluntary controlled schools, with county schools falling far behind in the quality of provision. Fewer than half the primary schools make good or better provision for spiritual development and in more than 10 per cent the provision is unsatisfactory.

This stark conclusion needs to be examined further. The OFSTED handbook directs inspectors to look for evidence of provision for spiritual development, in the opportunities for pupils to understand their beliefs and values and to reflect on meaningful experiences in their own lives. Collective worship and RE should provide most of these opportunities.

VALUES AND THE CURRICULUM

FIGURE 6.5
SPIRITUAL DEVELOPMENT BY TYPE OF SCHOOL – PRIMARY

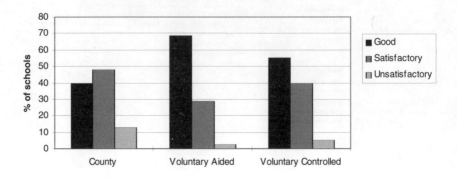

PROVISION FOR SPIRITUAL DEVELOPMENT - PRIMARY

FIGURE 6.6
SPIRITUAL DEVELOPMENT BY TYPE OF SCHOOL – SECONDARY

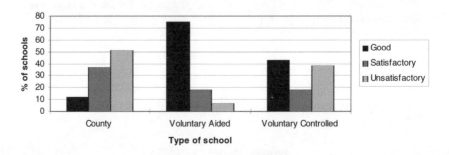

PROVISION FOR SPIRITUAL DEVELOPMENT - SECONDARY

COLLECTIVE WORSHIP

In three-quarters of all primary schools inspected it did appear that the schools were complying with the statutory requirement to provide a daily act of collective worship and there had been a 10 per cent increase since the previous year (see Figure 6.7).

The most noticeable feature of secondary schools is the extensive non-compliance in county schools (see Figure 6.8). However, the provision of collective worship does not necessary ensure that the spiritual development of pupils is promoted.

FIGURE 6.7
EVIDENCE OF NON-COMPLIANCE (COLLECTIVE WORSHIP) – PRIMARY

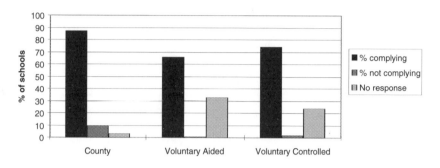

Provision of collective worship by type of school - primary

FIGURE 6.8
NON-COMPLIANCE WITH REQUIREMENT TO PROVIDE DAILY COLLECTIVE
WORSHIP – SECONDARY

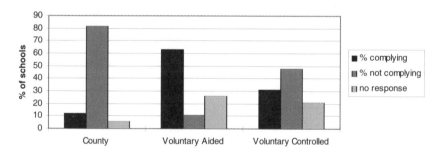

Provision of collective worship by type of school - secondary

The *quality* of collective worship is what contributes to spiritual development. Some of the best acts of worship were those where:

- careful planning across the year takes account of the school's aims, the curriculum, major festivals and events
- planning allows flexibility to insert important current issues (for example, the Dunblane massacre)
- pupils are involved in planning and presentation
- a Christian perspective is balanced with attention to other beliefs, allowing pupils to offer their own prayers and spiritual thinking

- those leading worship take account of the beliefs and non-belief of pupils and teachers, thus minimising the occurrences of withdrawal
- pupils are encouraged to think about their lives and beliefs and the needs of others at home and abroad
- teachers are encouraged to follow up ideas presented during the act of worship. However, for this continuity to be effective, teachers needed to attend the act of worship.

FIGURE 6. 9
PROVISION OF COLLECTIVE WORSHIP IN COUNTY AND VOLUNTARY SCHOOLS – PRIMARY

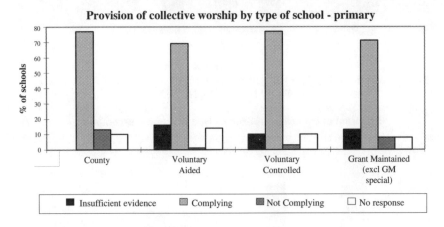

While most secondary schools do not provide *daily* worship, many of them do not compromise on quality, offering 'uplifting experiences' which draw on a range of media to promote spiritual development. While Voluntary Aided schools receive the highest praise, many of their forms of worship could be equally relevant for county-maintained schools. For example, Roman Catholic schools frequently include in their acts of worship prayer, meditation, talks, drama, music and art as well as the Mass.

Inspectors are particularly critical of acts of worship held in tutor groups as a means of meeting the statutory requirement. The practice is within the law but the content could rarely be called 'worship', and time-tabled occasions frequently do not take place. Some secondary schools offer a 'thought for the day' to be discussed and reflected upon in tutor groups, but, again, the quality of the discussion is as varied as the quality

FIGURE 6.10
PROVISION OF COLLECTIVE WORSHIP IN COUNTY AND VOLUNTARY
SCHOOLS – SECONDARY

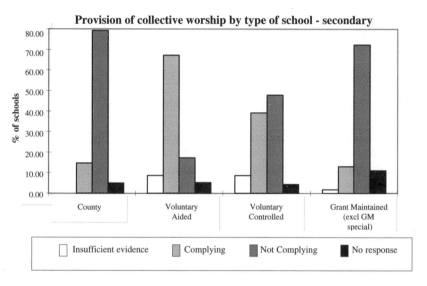

Provision of collective worship by type of school - secondary

of leadership of the group. For example, in one Science and Technology College, the thought for the day appeared on every computer in the school when the pupils logged on! From 60 sample reports, not one commented positively on collective worship, other than that held for the whole school, house or year groups.

Many reports on Catholic schools commented on the valuable contribution of chaplaincies to pupils' spiritual and general personal welfare. So positive are these comments that there may be value in investigating their possible adaptation to county-maintained schools.

SPIRITUAL DEVELOPMENT IN THE CURRICULUM

Understanding beliefs

A very substantial proportion of those primary and secondary schools included in the sample of 60 schools did provide opportunities for pupils to gain and develop an understanding of their own and other peoples' beliefs (see Figure 6.9). This was mainly provided through religious education although not exclusively. This exposure made a positive contribution to the pupils' spiritual development by exploring ultimate questions, for example about God and suffering. Nearly 80 per cent of primary schools, but fewer than half of secondary schools, comply fully with *the legal requirement* to provide religious education to all pupils. However the non-compliance in secondary schools is almost exclusively in the sixth form and there are many schools which failed to provide time at Key Stage 4 for the agreed syllabus to be taught (see Figure 6.10). Differences also exist in the levels of compliance between LEAs, but no LEA emerges as having very high rates of non-compliance.

The non-compliance with the obligation to provide religious education means that pupils are not provided with opportunities to enrich their spiritual development in a variety of ways. These might include visiting local places of worship to experience the atmosphere, to meet members of faith communities and to talk to them about their beliefs, to learn about Christianity and other faiths, forms of worship and contemplation, and to begin to understand how beliefs affect daily life. These opportunities make an important contribution to pupils' spiritual development, because they enhance pupils' awareness of the spiritual dimension of life, and encourage them to think about how people of different religions express their spirituality. This also raises the pupils' understanding that spirituality can affect the whole of life.

Promotion of values and beliefs

Most of the primary schools included in the sample surveyed not only teach about beliefs and values but go further in the *promotion of specific values* which are considered desirable for the school community. In five schools these values emphasised the worth of the non-material as well as the material, together with a purpose of life beyond personal success and the acquisition of material wealth. Whilst this overlaps with the criteria for moral development, the values promoted in these schools had a specifically spiritual dimension. The means adopted by the schools to ensure successful promotion included encouraging pupils to consider the wonders of creation, the joy and sadness of human creation (thus raising the 'religious' question of the possibility of a creator) and emphasising the importance of relationships and of the valuing of other people. This could be achieved by recognising the endeavours of individual pupils in a weekly assembly (raising the question of *why* individual pupils should be respected). Allowing time for pupils to think about their emotions and their contribution to human life (raising questions about how we are 'moved' and affected) can be parallelled with the development of a sense of community and the importance of mutual support (which overlaps with social development, although the sense of community with shared beliefs, values and solidarity, is also an important religious/spiritual concept). Most of these opportunities can be provided through collective worship and religious education.

Contemplation and inner peace

The OFSTED handbook (OFSTED, 2000) identifies reflection as contributing to spiritual development. The term is used widely by schools but it is never fully explained by them or in inspection reports. Spiritual development appears to cover three areas: opportunities for pupils to think about significant experiences, feelings, crises or what makes them happy or sad; opportunities to be calm, to put aside troubles and be at peace with themselves, others and, if appropriate, with God; and opportunities to think about others. The last of these is seen as a desirable outcome of the first two areas. Reflection is also seen as making a positive contribution to pupils' spiritual development where schools provide opportunities for pupils to reflect on emotional experiences, for example, through secular or religious poetry; or to reflect on human feeling, for example, in an RE lesson where pupils read David's lament over Saul and Jonathan and where they compare his feelings to their own on the loss of a friend. The pupils may develop a sense of awe and wonder in their responses to art work, such as an African cultural display, or by listening to music and the reading of Psalm 8 while viewing transparencies of space and the stars (RE/G/Sc). The pupils may also be encouraged to reflect when they follow their own religious observance as a result of careful timetabling and planning of extra-curricular activities. In RE there are many opportunities for contemplation but this does not hold for all other subjects in the secondary school curriculum. Some possibilities may include: in English with personal writing with a strong spiritual flavour; in English, history and geography with insights into human responses and emotions, or in drama with opportunities to think about themselves and others.

The list of opportunities and strengths can be matched with a range of weaknesses. This might include the absence of a shared understanding in the school of spiritual development and few planned opportunities to address it, or such opportunities as do exist being confined to collective worship and in no other curriculum area. Collective worship, on the other hand, may be planned informally and have neither a sense of occasion nor provide a reflective atmosphere with time for prayer. A significant weakness might be that the pupils have little encouragement to reflect upon their own meaningful experiences.

MORAL DEVELOPMENT

In all but two of the 60 schools included in the sample, the provision for pupils' moral development was good. The aims and ethos of the school were starting points for promoting moral development and were particularly strong when agreed with the parents.

Right and wrong

Where schools are making good provision for pupils' moral development there are clear statements, in the school prospectus or charter, of the moral values the school seeks to promote, such as honesty, fairness, hard work, care, consideration and respect. Teaching strategies and other clear disciplinary procedures emphasise school values and the distinction between right and wrong (for example, a sense of fair play is promoted through PE and games). Pupils are encouraged to think for themselves and to discuss a range of moral issues in RE, geography, history, English and science. In PE pupils are encouraged to make up their own rules for games. Teachers and other adults make a significant contribution in promoting moral principles through their interaction with each other and with pupils and, for example, in PE and sports, teachers provide good role models, successfully encouraging gender-opportunities as well as a sense of fair play.

Where the provision for moral development is good there is evidence of the school's moral values in practice. Schools are free of graffiti and litter, showing that the pupils have respect for themselves, others and their environment. The pupils' good behaviour during lunch and play-time illustrates their sense of responsibility and self-discipline. Further evidence is the agreement by the pupils of class rules to define what is right and wrong, as well as what is acceptable and unacceptable behaviour. The individual is respected through praise, recognition and occasional rewards for pupils of all abilities, in class or assembly, for good work, behaviour, attitude and contributions, thus reinforcing school values. Yet more evidence may be the support by the school of a range of charities including the National Children's Homes, the British Legion, Guide Dogs for the Blind and Children in Need. Weakness in the provision for moral development may be indicated by a behaviour and discipline policy and classroom lists of negotiated rules which are not always understood in practice by pupils, for example, lapses in behaviour which are not always recognised as such by pupils. Opportunities to address moral issues in the classroom are not always taken up or planned for and there is inconsistency among staff in applying the moral code, for example, assemblies may help pupils gain an understanding of the moral code but in some lessons there is no strategy for dealing with bad behaviour.

SOCIAL DEVELOPMENT

The provision for social development is good or better in more than 80 per cent of primary schools. Only 2 per cent were considered to have made unsatisfactory provision (see Figure 6.11 and 6.12).

FIGURE 6.11
PROVISION FOR OPPORTUNITIES FOR SOCIAL DEVELOPMENT – PRIMARY

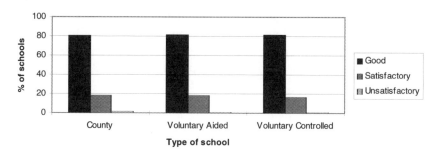

PROVISION FOR SOCIAL DEVELOPMENT - PRIMARY

FIGURE 6.12
PROVISION FOR OPPORTUNITIES FOR SOCIAL DEVELOPMENT –
SECONDARY

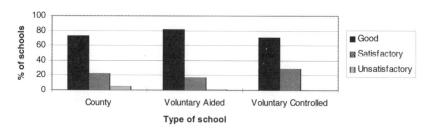

PROVISION FOR SOCIAL DEVELOPMENT

Developing interpersonal skills

Where the provision for social development is good or better, schools provide many opportunities for pupils to develop their interpersonal skills. These opportunities include paired or group work used to develop collaborative skills, together with sharing ideas and equipment. The participation in team games and after-school activities, for example, orchestra and chess club, was also a noteworthy feature.

Building a sense of community

Schools work very hard to develop in pupils a sense of belonging to a community and the rights and responsibilities involved. Many schools have extended pupils' social development by forging close links with the local community and in some cases, especially in small towns and villages, the school has become the cornerstone of the community. Successful schools use a variety of means to achieve this. Among them are organising events for the elderly, for example, a Christmas scheme whereby each pupil in the junior school is allocated a senior citizen from the local community with whom they and their parents make contact at Christmas and take gifts. In some schools the pupils become involved in local events, such as becoming aware of development plans for their town and participating in debates on key issues. Pupils can set up a village bottle-bank or devise and carry out a plan to clean the village pond. Other activities help to build up a sense of being part of a school community, such as residential visits and school camps.

DEVELOPING A SENSE OF RESPONSIBILITY

Many schools also make good provision for developing the pupils' sense of responsibility. Pupils may become holders of responsibility, acting as 'scavengers' to keep the school and grounds tidy and free from litter, or as classroom monitors, librarians, sports captains, house captains and prefects, or as monitors in charge of the organisation, storage and distribution of playground equipment. They could become members of the school council. Older children can help younger ones by helping reception pupils to dress themselves, and carry out other organisational tasks. Younger children can be helped to read or can be looked after at lunch time. Many primary schools have a strong environmental ethic. Pupils develop responsibility for the environment through managing school grounds, saving water and energy, recycling waste materials.

Schools promote these attitudes through environment-friendly policies, for example, buying recycled paper.

Few schools make poor provision for social development, but there are weaknesses. These may become apparent through insufficient provision of opportunities for pupils to work together or an uneven division of responsibilities with too few pupils holding responsibility over the majority. There may be insufficient opportunity for younger children to take responsibility and there may be too few opportunities for pupils to take responsibility for their own learning. There may also be a failure to develop appropriate skills in some pupils when interacting with others. The development of social skills is a prerequisite for progress and learning and, where social skills are lacking, disruptive behaviour distracts other pupils and hinders learning in the whole class.

CULTURAL DEVELOPMENT

Fewer than half of all the primary schools inspected made good or better provision for the pupils' cultural development, and in 10 per cent of schools the provision was unsatisfactory. In those schools where cultural development is taken seriously, lessons include a range of work based on paintings, pottery, music, literature, and poetry, and strive to develop pupils' cultural awareness and appreciation. Moreover in more than half of the schools where provision is satisfactory, there is an over-concentration on the pupils' own culture, and opportunities to explore and appreciate the cultures of others are lacking.

Most teachers stress the importance of all pupils understanding the traditions of the United Kingdom, but in the process there is a neglect of other cultures. A complication arises where schools have pupils from many cultures and 'their own culture' is not British culture. In these cases teachers are often unsure whether or not their role is to help all pupils to understand their own culture. This would be a practical impossibility in some schools where a wide range of cultures are represented.

UNDERSTANDING BRITISH AND EUROPEAN CULTURE ('THEIR OWN CULTURE' FOR MOST PUPILS)

In schools where the study of British and European culture is well developed the pupils are provided with widespread stimulation for detailed investigation. The local community, its history or architecture, etc., provide a basis for analysis and for comparisons between the past and the present. Visits are made to museums, such as the Victoria and Albert Museum in London and to art galleries to see the works of Western artists as well as to recognise the diversity of expression within a cultural tradition. Music and collective worship provide opportunities to become familiar with well-known pieces by composers in the Western tradition. Pupils also begin to understand the influence of the past through a well-organised history project, by comparing present-day culture with that of another age, for example Tudor times, through language, music and traditions. The learners may also take part in extra-curricular activities, for example, by visiting places of interest, such as historical or archaeological sites.

MULTI-CULTURAL UNDERSTANDING

Many schools are criticised for paying too little attention to other cultures. However those which do emphasise multi-cultural understanding often do so with great dedication. Pupils are encouraged to understand the beliefs, traditions and cultures of other people, regardless of their own perspective, in RE and geography. Other cultures are celebrated, for example, following a school refurbishment pupils performed a Chinese dance of welcome. Music from different cultures and traditions may be chosen for assemblies. One whole school assembly was organised and presented by a Hindu family from the school community. In other instances a variety of religious festivities were celebrated and the associated cultural traditions investigated. Pupils were also encouraged to read stories from different cultural traditions.

A FUTURE DIMENSION FOR SMSC

The provision of opportunities for pupils' spiritual, moral, social and cultural development is problematic for schools and inspectors. The law states that the curriculum *as a whole* should contribute to the pupils' spiritual, moral, social, cultural, mental and *physical* development. There is a widespread assumption that ALL subjects of the curriculum should promote equally the spiritual, moral, social and cultural development of pupils. There seems to be less concern for the physical. One reason for this is that, since the early 1990s, SMSC has become dissociated from mental (intellectual) and physical development and has assumed an identity of its own in isolation from its original context in the 1988 Education Reform Act.

It may be time to reconsider whether this is a reasonable interpretation, or a reasonable expectation. We do not expect RE and English, for example, to make the same contribution to pupils' physical development as PE. Why then should we expect D&T, IT and science to make the same contribution to spiritual development as RE, English, art and music? The term 'unsatisfactory' applied to all subjects which do not promote SMSC indicates that something is lacking. It could just as well be the case that fewer opportunities occur by the nature of these subjects. Further work on SMSC should make a *realistic* appraisal of the opportunities which *should* (rather than could) be presented by each subject area. It could be that, while 'satisfactory' and 'unsatisfactory' are appropriate judgements of the *curriculum's* contribution to SMSC, they are less appropriate in relation to all subjects. Such an approach would define more clearly the context for the provision of SMSC and potentially enable inspectors to make more precise assessments of the degree to which SMSC development is provided for within the school curriculum, both overt and hidden.

REFERENCES

OFSTED (2000) *Inspecting Schools.* London, OFSTED.

Part III:

A Wider View of Education in Values

7

THE MARKET-FRAMED UNIVERSITY: THE NEW ETHICS OF THE GAME

Robert Cowen

And they write innumerable books; being too vain and distracted for silence; seeking every one after his own elevation, and dodging his emptiness. (Eliot, 1969, p. 158)

THE UNIVERSITY, AND MAYBE UNIVERSITY SYSTEMS: ENCLAVES AND OTHER METAPHORS

One of the classical models of the university is that of Wilhelm von Humboldt (Rohrs, 1995). His vision of the university – revitalised in the thinking of Karl Jaspers (Walters, 1996) – defines its external relations; its epistemological assumptions and thus its external and internal evaluative procedures; its internal hierarchies and thus its internal professional relations.

In its external relations with the State the Humboldtian university, by a sociological *leger-de-main*, remains independent. Historically, in its practice, it was granted major freedoms in Germany. By the 1890s (as well as, most dramatically, in the 1930s) those freedoms had collapsed under economic and political pressures. But in the original vision the Humboldtian university was to be an enclave, with its own mission. The enclave was created and initially safeguarded by the State (Rohrs, 1995, pp. 24–33; Gellert, 1993).

Epistemologically, the university was to pursue *Bildung* and *Wissenschaft* – forms of education, understanding and science based in a particular interpretation of the rational. The pursuit of knowledge and truth was subject to its own principles which were internal to academic disciplines and the pursuit was untrammelled by state or religious interference (Walters, 1996, pp. 97–8). Following Jaspers, Walters indicates the university is:

> ...akin to a 'State within a state' that is ever in conflict with state power and political manoeuvrings. For the university ideally controls the state through the power of truth and not through force. This is why the professor must seek the truth as neither civil servant nor corporate member, neither politician nor political propagandist. While Jaspers acknowledges a cooperative relationship between the university and the state, his is a minimalist view of state intervention confined to a purely supervisory administrative capacity and to the guarantee of the university's right to academic freedom uncontrolled by external political, philosophical or religious ideologies.

The professional internal relations of the university were to be dominated by the Professor. Such Professors, as heads of disciplines, were largely independent; quasi-monarchs subject only to the checks and balances of criticism by debate in the university and the judgement of the (international) scholarly community after publication. Professorial relations with colleagues – *Dozents* and students – were hierarchical, those of master (sic) and apprentice. Peer judgement, dominated by the Professor, was the criterion of quality. Evaluative procedures were thus based on clear principles of exclusion. The models of professional relations were those of a Guild, and admission to the Guild was marked by the *Habilitation*, which might or might not lead to an academic position (Gellert, 1993).

Thus overall, the insulation of State and university was deliberately marked by a carefully structured ethic of separation and political neutrality (on both sides). The ethic carried by the epistemological vision of the university was that of research and truth-seeking, an ancient commitment but reformulated since the days of the medieval university under the impact of the principles of rationality celebrated by the Enlightenment. The evaluation ethic was similar to that of apprenticeship within the guild – which was one of the original models of the medieval university itself (Ridder-Symoens, 1992).

There are multiple variants, earlier and later, on the Humboldt model – for example the ideas of Locke, Arnold and Newman in England, or Jefferson in the USA (in his Plan for the Diffusion of Knowledge in the

State of Virginia). But there are no clear models of the market-framed university. However there are a number of practices from which such a model can be deduced, notably the practices of the contemporary English university whose construction is marked by currently evolving policy, and also by legislation.

In theory a market-framed university is inserted into a double-market. In the internal market, it competes with other universities for prestige and repute – but this prestige and repute is marked by public measuring instruments (such as the National Research Assessment in England). Externally the market-framed university is located within a competitive financial universe, which means that it must attract external clients (students, research foundation monies) to guarantee itself a continuing existence (Cowen, 1991).

Thus the market-framed university requires managing – it must monitor its progress in both internal and external markets and adjust its behaviour within evaluation cycles to maintain market repute, market share and market reward.

Externally, the relations of the market-framed university are initially dominated by the State (central or federal) because it is the State which deliberately sets up the rules of the game. It is the State which defines criteria by which performance will be judged. The State creates a dependency relation in the university (normally within the rhetoric of 'quality control'). The State is the rule-maker; the university the competitor. The social space – the enclave of the Humboldtian university – is invaded and the political and economic distance between the university and the State collapses; more precisely it is deliberately collapsed by the laws and agencies of the State to create an ethic of competition and efficiency.

Epistemologically, the market-framed university must deliver marketable, saleable, pragmatically useful knowledge. The market-framed university exists within a knowledge market, and it must respond to the demands of its clients and customers (for example, students; research funders). The knowledge production of the university must also be measurable – otherwise performance cannot be judged. Thus managerial decisions must be taken about the differential worth of knowledge products, against rules and criteria which are externally mandated.

In the market-framed university the professional relations which are of major significance within the university are those between the managers and the academic producers (the professorate and contract researchers); and the managers and internal clients (the students); and the managers and external clients (e.g. research agencies). This pattern of relations subordinates academics to rules of expected performance. Typically the rules are explicitly stated, as if in a contract.[1] Evaluative procedures are thus placed in the public domain, a domain dominated by the management system. The managers in turn are necessarily responsive to external rules which define their own successful performance as a management group. The evaluative rules shift from the personalised judgements of academic authorities (the professors) to universalised rules: measuring, through standardised and bureaucratic rules, the flow of scholarly production, the processes of teaching and customer satisfaction.

Thus the external ethic shifts, in Lyotard's word, to 'performativity' (Cowen, 1996a) as decided by national rules. The epistemological ethic shifts to the production of measurable and pragmatically useful knowledge (as demanded by customers and clients). The professional relations of those working inside the university are subordinated to management organisation. Traditional academic culture – of the sort envisioned by Humboldt and Jaspers – is displaced, and explicit relations of contract dominate (and replace) those of obligation.

Such an ideal-typical model of a market-framed university can be quickly placed against a range of international experience which includes Australia, Canada and England (Cowen, 1996b). It is important to note that the cases do not suggest that everywhere the market-framed university is the same. In the United States, much of the intervention by the State comes at the level of the individual states, such as New York or California (Franzosa, 1996). Similarly in Canada the intervention by the State often is at the level of the Provinces (Mallea, 1996). But in both countries a *national* crisis has been recognised through major Reports – and currently the concern is about the performativity of the university (and higher education) system as a whole. Of the three cases England (and the United Kingdom) is, however, the most extreme. England now has national rules, national financing patterns, and national results, as these are defined by national agencies on a national measurement cycle of four years. England has by far the most comprehensive (and cumbersome) system for measuring performativity.

However, in all three cases, and taking into account variations in the mix and meld of ideas from Jefferson and Humboldt, Locke and Arnold, Ryerson and Dewey, as well as the histories of the details of international borrowing and influence (such as the influence of Scottish models in the USA and Canada), significant shifts away from the Humboldt model have occurred. In all three places, university systems have been affected by state intervention, concepts of 'performativity' and the device of market-framing. In all three national systems there has been an increased stress on 'managing' the crisis. That is, with different emphases and within different cultural mixes, the (proper) management of the university has become a way of solving the crisis. This is a new idea, especially for England, and the speed of change has been dramatic (Scott, 1995, p. 61).

It is worth pausing to ask if this form of the politicisation of the university has the attributes which have been so dramatically sketched for politicising in general where politicising 'is the engagement of proponents of particular ideological fashion to dominate others' (Fuller, 1996, pp. 129 and 131):

> They include lust for change, boredom with conversation, a preference for activism over reflection, a taste for melodramatic tension and 'creative problem solving', quests for the authentic life through policy formation, rejection of tradition for fear of the influence of the past, demand for diversity as a function of a desire for ultimate homogeneity....

The answer is, 'probably not' – because if the matter were that clear-cut, then opposition would already have become vociferous. But the question is still important. We are all accustomed to 'management' and 'being managed' now. It is worth wondering why, and trying to sketch some of the ethical dilemmas in which men and women, of goodwill and high principle, are caught in the new university structures in which they work.

MANAGEMENT, AND EVEN MANAGEMENT SYSTEMS

All management systems are message systems. They define and transmit rules about appropriate professional or job-related behaviour. They define the correct relations of those managed, to each other, and to the management system, but they differ in what they stress. They may embed hierarchy, as in the classical Fordist model, or they may deliberately seek flatter hierarchies (e.g. in certain design workshops or in the cutting edge of the software branches of the computer industry) as ways to maximise creativity and performance. Management systems are themselves capable of metaphorical definition, for example, as bureaucracies, as webs, as organisms, as machines (Morgan, 1986). Management systems are also externally framed. They arise within particular economic, political, cultural and ideological contexts.

Perhaps (in a university) they embody the notion of a community, of a self-governing republic of scholars; or they may embody a notion of efficient productivity as in a major industrial combine (such as Ford Motors or IBM). Models of guild, partnership or college involve different assumptions about hierarchy to those of corporation, industrial conglomerate, or firm.

The 'guild' model takes its genesis in one notion of *Gemeinschaft* – a fictive community which, while hierarchical, functions through face-to-face reactions, a sense of communal identity, and a principle of equality through the rite of admission.

The 'corporation' model takes its genesis in one notion of *Gesellschaft* – a pattern of specific functional relations marked by neutrality of effect and by obligations of contract. The pattern of relations is determined by written communication, social distance in managerial relations and patterns of inequality marked by formal positions within a management grid.

The two models thus express broad affective *or* narrow instrumental professional relations, obligations to a collective *or* obligations to a management group. They express a different ethic of (social) relation: personalised or depersonalised; institutionalised charismatic or institutionalised legal–rational; evaluation of conduct character and manner (and some aspects of performance) or performativity on specific explicit universal criteria; applicable *sine ire et studio*.

In the corporation model, the ideological is often succinctly expressed in a Mission Statement, and is specified in detail in the instruments of governance, such as a Board of Directors, Senior Management – or in the university in the dreadful phrase, 'senior academic staff'. The Mission Statement in the 'corporation' is the ideological mediator between the external and the internal. The practical mediator between the external and the internal is finance. The internal ideological *and* practical mediator is a notion of performance, embodying as it does notions of product, quality and fulfilment of mission.

The two models thus incorporate different ethics (and sociologies) of evaluation, observation and information.

In the guild model the surveillance is personal, intimate, reputational and of the whole person. Surveillance works best if it is internalised, for example, as in the internalisation of a professional ethic.

In the corporation model, surveillance is depersonalised, distanced, defined by written rules and is of the performative *part* of the person. Surveillance is assumed to work best if it is externalised, i.e. routinised in time, done through explicit universal criteria and subject to management definition.

In the 'guild', the collection of information is irregular, personalised and anecdotal. In the 'corporation', the collection of information is systematic, regular, quantified and centralised bureaucratically. Corporate management cannot occur without information, and the time span for action is short: adaptations are made within an unstable external universe. In the guild model, a stable external universe is assumed.

In the 'guild', management is in, by and through the fictive community, which is also its own 'diplomatic corps' – it deals with its own external relations. In the 'corporation', the fictive community (for example, of university scholars) is subordinated to 'the management'. The external relations of the community of university scholars (for example, applications for research funding or with the media) are filtered and controlled through precise mechanisms, such as a Research Officer or a Public Relations Department.

The consequence is that, in the 'corporation', surveillance of performance, of external relations and of sub-group activity becomes pan-optical (Harrison, 1994). The information system itself is set up to achieve this goal – and requires the co-operation of those under surveillance. The system finally works smoothly when the management's ideas of information flow and performativity are internalised by those under surveillance, that is, when members of the corporation begin to produce adaptive behaviour without the need to refresh their memories of the written-out rules of performance. Books are more important than edited books; reviews should not be written, or should be given a very low priority, as a *personal* commitment perhaps. Full internalisation of the rules means that the management system is working well: individuals control their own tendencies to deviate from the explicit, and now routinised, rules of performance.

Such a management system is infinitely adjustable and tuneable. Smaller and smaller pieces of information can be collected, more and more surveillance can be devised. It is a matter of technique – good computers and a well-structured (and restructurable) educational management information system are, however, essential. There is much to manage.

In England, the current and emerging arrangements for the surveillance of pedagogy, research performance and evaluation of both staff and students are in modalities, which permit the *factorisation* of performance. Knowledge, in taught courses and even in doctoral research training, is modularised. Research performance is broken down into measurable units: books, edited books, articles (academic), articles (professional), 'other public output' and so on. Both students and staff are evaluated on a piece-rate basis. Overall, there are not merely tendencies to separate teaching and research and general education in 'the university'; there is also a tendency to separate teaching itself into specific acts of competence (clarity of specification of aims of courses, 'relevant' bibliography, mode of presentation of material) and to separate the research act into sub-categories of differentially valued performances. Evaluation is thereby simplified and factorised.

The current policy stress is on constructing pedagogies and research profiles that can be 'managed', within a specific concept of what management is. The older vision of the university is being lost sociologically, in the contemporary mechanics of management. This is, not least, because the management of our universities is being socially constructed under heavy external pressures. It may be asked whether these pressures, and the social location of the contemporary market-framed universities of England are putting those who manage them in an ethically impossible, and even a historically dangerous, position. There are some awkward dilemmas facing the university, for which present management systems, post-Jarrett, may not be appropriate.

CONCLUSION

The market-framed university has a specific genesis: in the declarations of a contemporary national crisis – in a number of nations, but notably England – and in the ideologies of the solutions for that crisis. 'The University' is being redefined within, and refined to become part of, those solutions. The context of those solutions includes at least three important dimensions. The international world is seen as primarily economic; 'the University' is seen as a set of national institutions of unequal 'quality'; and solutions can be 'managed'. Each of these assumptions, if taken too seriously, carries its own weaknesses and creates its own dangers.

The international world, on several criteria and on several analyses, is indeed being 'globalised', economically and there is some evidence that the terms of international economic competition are to be understood through the idea of a world knowledge-economy (OECD, 1987). National research and development structures are under reform in Australia, Britain, Canada and elsewhere. In this context the question to be asked is not whether universities should be encouraged, especially by democratically mandated governments, to contribute to a redefinition of the skill base and research potential of the nation-state. The question is how much of the university should be so technicised, within a given set of national rules for performativity.

Universities have historically provided an alternative voice to those of the Church and the State. They have done this on the basis of their intellectual independence – their academic freedom if you will – and they have provided a critical alternative voice, distinctive even from those defences of freedoms which an independent media system can offer. The contemporary crisis – globalisation and the relative increase in powerlessness of the 'nation-State' – is not merely an economic crisis. It is a cultural one, which requires historical, sociological, anthropological, cultural and philosophical analysis. If the social and human sciences are impoverished by technicisation – by performativity, by pragmatism, by an excessive concern for the immediate and the useful – then one of the defences of nations to understand what is happening to them will be dramatically weakened.

Thus the question becomes one of cultural defence through the university's traditional involvement with intellectual openness – and the point of that openness and breadth of vision: an improved *understanding* of contemporary social, economic and political processes. Emancipatory rather than technical-empirical knowledge carries, however, a price. The price is how much will societies pay for an enclave partly devoted to the non-immediate; or will they prefer the conscious decision that universities transmute into 'think-tanks' funded by clients with knowledge construction driven by such an external market? Equally, the question is whether university leaders (not managers) see the need for such an enclave and if they do whether they can create appropriate internal structures (probably involving real resources 'lost' and time not used in increasing public ratings of performance) in their universities.

In a different age, and after a different crisis, a version of this point was stressed in the thinking of Jaspers, 'following the principle of preventing absolutisation of any single function of the university' (Salamun, 1996, p. 51):

> For Jaspers, the idea of the university includes three main functions which stimulate each other with a plurality of impulses. These functions are: research, transmission of learning, and education to culture. All three constitute free, intellectual university life. This life degenerates if the university is restricted to a mere research institution, to a mere institution of professional training, or to a mere cultural centre of general education.

In England, we are currently close to a new absolutism (of the 'market idea') and we are close to permitting a glorification of the 'research university' as representing all that we might become.

The emphasis on the aspiration to become a 'research university' is comprehensible. As Burton Clark has demonstrated at brilliant length, this, in the United States, is where the money, the prestige and the national and international repute moves to and, for a time, rests (Clark, 1993). It is too soon to tell what is happening to the new mass university system of England, or even of the United Kingdom. However there have already been comments that the 'old' universities have a powerful start in what is tending to be seen as a race between institutions (Scott, 1995). Clearly if you are a manager of, or within, a university it is your managerial duty to get your institution on the escalator of excellence, before mobility within the evaluation system becomes more difficult as oligopolistic rigidities consolidate. That, as a manager, is simply playing the game by the given rules, with a touch of intelligent anticipation.

The difficulty with the game – and its ethic – is that it is a national game; and it is a rather trivial game for a nation to be playing. A book may indeed be a book (provided it is 80 pages long, preferably published externally to the university, and has an ISBN number). But the historic questions remain: does the book have international currency; does it break the boundaries of a subject (or invent a new one); and does it – on international criteria – redefine the nature of our understanding of an intellectual domain or mark a new *Verstehen* in our grasp of the changing (social, economic, political, or even physical) universe? I recognise that our national evaluation system says that there are departments or institutions of 'international excellence'; and that there is also a concept of domestic ('national') excellence, which it is apparently possible for an institution to fail to reach. But the game is not merely taking up too much valuable time in universities, it is also a domestic game. It is sorting out *within the national system* the weak from the strong players. Certainly this is a Herculean labour of a fairly unpleasant kind, but it is the wrong game. If you want national research universities – 'our' universities – to compete in a globalised international knowledge economy with MIT, CalTech, and so on, then create them. Set up an international, rather than a domestic, game.

However, at the present moment, we as universities cannot play such a game. The current sociological processes of English higher education speak to tighter and tighter mechanistic controls over the measurement of research (including soft-money funding and Ph.D. graduation rates), over pedagogic process and the measurement of teaching quality and over the (indirect) career rating of the people who manage our universities. The result is that we – as institutions and as individual academics – are forced to be domestically oriented in our performativities, bureaucratic in our behaviours in research production and course organisation and obsessed with the short-term opportunities and punishments offered by four-year cycles of performance. We are consolidating the university as if it is a managerial locus, a locale, a *finalite*, amoebic.

Thus we are missing the point. The university is attentuating (Cowen, 1996a). It is more and more dispersed. It is increasingly dispersed financially and pedagogically. It is dispersed in its recruitment and use of staff, and in its recruitment and subsequent relations with students. It is increasingly spread wide in its research space and in its research–contract relations (Skilbeck and Connell, 1996).

It must become more so; not least in a globalised international knowledge economy. The hierarchies must become flatter. In England recently they have become steeper. 'Management' seems to have become tighter and more efficient. It probably has. But it is the wrong style of management for the attenuated university. I suggest we have a national crisis, in the new international world. We have failed in our *Verstehen* – we have picked the wrong metaphor of management.

The metaphor is not, correctly, that of a machine; even a machine controlled by a managerial brain. The useful metaphor is that of a web, a network (Morgan, 1986). The question is what kind of pedagogies, evaluation styles, epistemological assumptions and sources of creativity are appropriate in a webbed or networked academic universe. And in which style(s) should you, and do you, manage a metaphorical web? Certainly not by the domestication and nationalisation of the piece-rate production and the reward systems of classical Fordism, even if panoptical supervision techniques have become efficient.

The metaphor is out of time, precisely because it is too much in tune with older times. A university should not be. It should be in front of the times especially, in the words of Ernest Boyer, in the scholarships of discovery, integration, application and teaching. This means it should have some safeguarded space to ask its own questions, including critical ones, to define its own performance against *international* criteria, and to resist suggestions that its best service to society is to be at the service of governments. It should be in front of the times, including in its management structures. The model of managements should not be infinitely responsive to external pressures and should not be trapped in a cult of efficiency (Callahan, 1962), as if universities were the public schools of America in the first half of this century or English schools in the first half of the next?

If the metaphors of guild and corporation and management will not do any longer for 'the university', maybe it is time we looked again at metaphors of leadership, quality and, beginning from Boyer, of scholarship.

NOTES

1. I am indebted to Crispin Jones for this *aperçu*.

REFERENCES

Callahan, R.E. (1962) *Education and the Cult of Efficiency: A Study of the Social Forces that have shaped the Administration of Public Schools*. Chicago, University of Chicago Press.

Clark, B.R. (ed.) (1993) *The Research Foundations of Graduate Education: Germany, Britain, France, United States, Japan*. Berkeley, University of California Press.

Cowen, R. (1991) 'The Management and Evaluation of the Entrepreneurial University: The Case of England', *Higher Education Policy*, 4(3).

Cowen, R. (1996a) 'Performativity, Post-modernity and the University', *Comparative Education*, 33(2).

Cowen, R. (ed.) (1996b) *The Evaluation of Higher Education Systems: World Yearbook of Education 1996*. London, Kogan Page.

Eliot, T.S. (1969) *The Complete Poems and Plays of T.S. Eliot*. London and Boston, Faber & Faber.

Franzosa, S. (1996) 'The Evaluation of the Higher Education System in the United States of America', in R. Cowen (ed.), *The Evaluation of Higher Education Systems: World Yearbook of Education 1996*. London, Kogan Page.

Fuller, T. (1996) 'The University and the Experience of Transcendence', in G. Walters (ed.) *The Tasks of Truth: Essays on Karl Jaspers's Idea of the University*. Frankfurt am Main, Peter Lang.

Gellert, C. (1993) 'The German Model of Research and Advanced Education', in B.R. Clark (ed.), *The Research Foundations of Graduate Education: Germany, Britain, France, United States, Japan*. Berkeley, University of California Press.

Harrison, M. J. (1994) 'Quality Issues in Higher Education: A Post-modern Phenomenon?', in G.D. Doherty (ed.), *Developing Quality Systems in Higher Education*. London, Routledge.

Mallea, J. (1996) 'The Evaluation of the Higher Education System in Canada', in R. Cowen (ed.), *The Evaluation of Higher Education Systems: World Yearbook of Education 1996*. London, Kogan Page.

Morgan, G. (1986) *Images of Organization*. Beverly Hills, CA, Sage.

OECD (1987) [Taylor, W.] *Universities Under Scrutiny*. Paris, OECD.

Ridder-Symoens, H. de (ed.) (1992) *A History of the University in Europe: Volume One, Universities in the Middle Ages*. Cambridge, Cambridge University Press.

Rohrs, R. (1995) *The Classical German Concept of the University and its Influence on Higher Education in the United States*. Frankfurt am Main, Peter Lang.

Salamun, K. (1996) 'The Concept of Liberality in Jaspers' Philosophy and the Idea of the University', in G. Walters (ed.), *The Tasks of Truth: Essays on Karl Jaspers's Idea of the University*. Frankfurt am Main, Peter Lang.

Scott, P. (1995) *The Meanings of Mass Higher Education*. Buckingham, SRHE & Open University Press.

Skilbeck, M. and Connell, H. (1996) 'International Education from the Perspective of Emergent World Regionalism: The Academic, Scientific and Technological Dimension', in P. Blumenthal, C. Goodwin, A. Smith and U. Teichler (eds), *Academic Mobility in a Changing World: Regional and Global Trends.* London, Jessica Kingsley.

Walters, G. (ed.) (1996) *The Tasks of Truth: Essays on Karl Jaspers's Idea of the University.* Frankfurt am Main, Peter Lang.

8

INSTITUTIONAL VALUES AND PERSONAL DEVELOPMENT

Richard Pring

There are several problems I want to address in this chapter which seem relevant to the teaching of values in our schools. First, there is the problem of 'which values?', given the religious and moral pluralism which characterises our society. Second, there is the problem of moral authority: by virtue of what knowledge and expertise do teachers or politicians lay claims to authority on what values to teach? Third, there is the problem of reconciling whatever social consensus their exists in a school or institution with the serious exploration and thinking of the learner – who may not appreciate or wish to subscribe to those 'agreed' values. Fourth, there is the problem of how best those values might effectively be taught – both the teaching methods and the appropriate teaching context.

I do not intend to address these problems systematically. But they all create puzzles which are the background to my thinking. I shall divide this chapter as follows.

First, I examine briefly the commonly recognised problems arising from disagreement over what values should be promoted.

Second, I examine the implication of this for personal development.

Third, I draw conclusions about the institutional framework for personal development.

WHAT VALUES? LIVING WITH PLURALISM

There is disagreement within society over the values which should be promoted by schools – except at a level which is so abstract that it permits a wide range of irreconcilable differences. Think awhile of such old moral issues as the practice of abortion, contraception, pre-marital sex, homosexuality, lying successfully to the Inland Revenue, using violence to achieve legitimate objectives, using weapons of war which kill indiscriminately, eating meat, destroying the environment, restraining people who wish to commit suicide.

The list could go on for a long time. The point is that, on substantive moral matters, there is profound disagreement within schools which reflects disagreement at a wider societal level. And this clearly raises problems about the teaching of moral judgement or the promotion of particular values. If one is to teach moral judgement and values, then there are clearly difficult decisions to be made about which values or about whose expertise or authority might be invoked in order for a decision to be made.

It is important to reflect on the nature of the disagreement. There is within society disagreement over a range of matters which have nothing to do with values. Scientists disagree. Economists disagree. And people disagree with scientists and economists – having previously experienced the errors in their judgements. However, so the argument goes, in these non-value disagreements, one can see how differences might be reconciled *if* one proceeds in a particular way or *if* efforts are made to collect the relevant data. One can also see how, in retrospect, a particular belief (in science, say, or in economics) was erroneous. As a result of argument or of new evidence or of further experiment, one recognises the errors of earlier beliefs. Furthermore, there is development within science and economics as a result of such disagreements and their reconciliation. There is thus an accumulation of knowledge, a development of the discipline, and the recognition of experts and authorities who are internal to the arguments, experimentation, and data collection. But this does not seem to be the case where questions of values are concerned. There does not seem to be a recognised way of resolving differences. There does not appear to be the accumulation and development of knowledge. And, as Plato argued when he considered whether virtue could be taught, there do not seem to be the moral experts. There are several different kinds of response to this particular difficulty – I shall mention but three.

First, there is the view that some people (by virtue of their superior upbringing, intelligence and education) do have a special insight into these moral matters – just as Plato's guardians in the Republic might, through careful selection and an education in mathematics and philosophy, acquire the moral insight required of a philosopher king who could then, with wisdom, direct the lives of others. Such people – the 'clerisy' referred to by Coleridge – would have an intuitive understanding of what was objectively good. Moral education would, of course, help others to gain that insight, but would also, where that insight is not acquired, nurture those virtues of obedience and of respect according to which the moral waiverers defer to the wiser counsels of the moral experts.

Although such 'intuitionist' theories of morals are no longer fashionable amongst philosophers, as they once were (see Ross, 1939), they do sometimes prevail within powerful religious traditions or indeed within the unreflective practice of many schools and of those who govern them. Statements about the virtues of patriotism, about honesty in all matters concerning property or about not taking advantage of the weak seem intuitively true to some, but (self-evidently) not so to everyone.

A second position would be one where, given the unconvincingness of self-evident truths or intuitive knowledge, there is a distinct 'moral rationality' – a way of proceeding in moral disagreements (just as there is in scientific matters) – which, if faithfully adhered to, would enable one to arrive at the moral truth and to show where other people are wrong. Wilson *et al.*'s (1967) *An Introduction to Moral Education* argued for such a position, following the work of Hare (1952). Indeed, it was Hare's view that, if only one were prepared to argue correctly for long enough and not be distracted by countervailing emotions, one would be able to reach a rational conclusion and reconcile differences of opinion.

The criticism of this position, succinctly argued by Han (1996), is that, although there may be some very general rules for moral argument to be adhered to if conclusions are to be rationally attained, such general rules are too few and too abstract to overcome the range of differences validly and honestly held by those who disagree with each other. Such logical rules tell only part of the story. People begin from different premises. Key concepts (for example murder or stealing or injustice) are open to development, and have somewhat different connotations given the different 'forms of life' to which they are applied. Take an example. It is difficult to see how, simply from the application of certain general rules of logic or through an agreed method, people with very different views on abortion would disown their differences and happily reach the same conclusion. Moral argument and reflection simply do not seem to be of that kind. People start from different premises (let us say, a religious tradition which, first, upholds the absolute sanctity of human life, and, second, ascribes to the embryo already a distinctively human form of life); they give priority to different competing 'goods' (for example, personal fulfilment as measured by satisfaction or pleasure, as opposed to preservation of life in general); their concepts cover different ranges of instances (as in the case where the concept of 'human' may or may not extend to those brain damaged or the unborn).

A third position, therefore, and one which is quite common, is to say there is not – nor can there be, however exhaustive the argument – agreement in society upon 'the good life' or the list of values which can be comprehensively promoted. (This, by the way, does not entail the relativism which the chief executive of SCAA and now the chief inspector of schools see [wrongly] all around them. It is quite consistent to believe, at one and the same time, that the moral views one holds [as, say, over abortion] are correct, and thus those that hold contradictory views are wrong, and that there is no ultimately rational way of demonstrating the truth to those who do not share the same 'form of life' or begin from the same 'world view' or premise.) Given this irreconcilable set of differences, one might make the following move. There cannot be agreement on substantive moral issues – on, if you like, the 'good life to be pursued' – but there can be agreement on those conditions which are essential for living with these differences and for disagreeing sensibly and constructively over such matters. There may not be agreement on the moral values, but there can be on the political virtues which enable one to live in a pluralist society. Such political virtues would include 'tolerance'.

That is one mark of liberalism – an espousal of moral differences and the creation of the political and institutional conditions in which those differences might be an enrichment rather than an impoverishment of a distinctively human life. Given the inevitable difference of view, what sort of society should one create in which one might not only tolerate but support such differences? Clearly to answer that question was the philosophical agenda of Rawls (1993). But it is reflected at a much more practical level in the kind of work which one sees in schools where teachers provide the forum for discussion on those matters which mean so much to how life should be lived (for example, with regard to relations between the sexes, the use of violence, domestic obligations and relationships, respect for other religions and ethnic groups, and so on) but where, at the same time, they refrain 'from imposing their own views'. There is a commitment to 'respect for persons' such that the pupils' views (however wrongly conceived the teacher might regard them) receive an equal airing.

Such regular and widespread practice has been formalised into a distinctive curriculum package, referred to as 'values clarification', in which the teacher, quite non-judgementally, helps the pupils systematically to reflect upon the values they hold (see Simon, 1972 and Rath, 1966).

As an interim conclusion, therefore, one can say that there are apparently irreconcilable differences within society, and thus within schools, over the idea of the good life, over what counts as a virtuous way of living, and thus over the values to be promoted. Without subscribing to any form of relativism, one might *as educators* face this difficulty by arguing for certain institutional conditions – certain agreed political virtues – which will not only accept but positively welcome these moral disagreements.

PERSONAL DEVELOPMENT WITHIN A PLURALIST SOCIETY

There are at least two possible objections to this point of view both of which have implications for practice – although that might not be immediately apparent.

First, disagreement at the level of specific rules does not entail disagreement at the level of general moral principle. Thus, abstract though they may seem, certain general principles (with their associated virtues) could be argued for as necessarily part of any recognisable form of moral life. One might cite, for example, a concern for truth where argument and debate are seriously engaged in or a respect for persons or a concern for justice, all with their appropriate intellectual and moral virtues and dispositions.

It could be pointed out that this does not take us far. The connection between 'respect for persons' and concrete and specific rules of behaving towards other people is rarely clear, but it is not vacuous, for the specific rules and prescriptions are instances and interpretations of such general principle – such interpretations reflecting wider understandings and beliefs about human nature. And, under the influence of such general principles, one raises questions, seeks further explanations, tries to make explicit the underlying concept of 'being a person'. Indeed, such general principles are a kind of abstraction from a living and concrete tradition, and are necessarily embodied within a particular form of life and practice. But, and this is important, such forms of life – and thus such embodiments of general principle – are never static. They change through reflection, through deliberation and criticism, in the light of other developments in knowledge or of changing economic and social needs.

A second objection is that the distinction – between moral and political virtues, between a diversity of 'comprehensive goods' and an agreed political framework in which that diversity is tolerated and welcomed – is much greyer and more blurred than its liberal exponents would acknowledge. For the *particular* notion of justice which underpins it is itself contestable. It is part of the form of life which is one amongst many that people might argue for. Even if one were to argue for a democratic political framework, in which differences of value and moral purpose might happily co-exist, as the political and moral *sine qua non* of a tolerant society, there are many different interpretations of the democratic ideal and of its expression in institutional arrangements. In other words, the political framework itself is necessarily, along with the moral ends which the citizens freely choose, open to discussion, criticism, deliberation and change. It is itself one of the several contestable parts of the 'good life' which the liberal society needs constantly to question and reformulate.

From this, certain things would seem to follow.

First, part of the human condition is that of uncertainty as to the ends or purposes which are worth pursuing. There is no agreement, nor could there conceivably be, on the specific values which the nurturing and education of children should serve.

Second, and following from this, there are not the moral experts who have the authority to lay down in detail what those specific ends should be – what exactly is the position that each and everyone should adopt on those matters which affect so profoundly the quality of relationship which one enters into or the style of life to be pursued.

Third, any point of view in such matters embodies a set of valuings which contain implicitly wider understandings about society, human nature, etc. Each of us, in that respect, participates in traditions which are largely implicit in the way we see things but which pick out the significant from the insignificant.

Fourth, however, such traditions change over time – through their failure to meet new and challenging changes in, say, the economic or technological developments within society or through experience of other traditions or through criticism found in literature, art and the conversations with others.

Fifth, therefore, at the centre of the education, broadly conceived, of the next generation must be the acknowledgement that in those matters which are of most importance – the kind of relationships to be entered into, the style of life to be adopted, the way of resolving conflicts of principle, the recognition of oneself as a person of worth and of dignity, the value to be placed upon particular objects and activities – there is an openness of judgement, a continuous argument between the generations, a range of uncertainties with which each and everyone has to engage, and eventually come to a decision no matter how provisional.

There are many aspects of personal development which one might point to, but possibly the most important is that capacity to engage seriously with those uncertainties about the quality of life worth pursuing – with all its ramifications with regard to relationships, obligations, aspirations, modes of living and dispositions to be nurtured. That capacity requires certain virtues or dispositions, certain strengths of character, but above all the tools to enter into the reflection and thought, into the debate and conversation which addresses such matters. For it is important to remember that, although each must necessarily and ultimately take responsibility for the way of living chosen, the reflective and serious consideration of the possibilities is rooted in a *public* debate – one that is conducted through literature and the arts, through the writing and the interpretation of history, through the social and economic analysis of our institutions, through the deliberation of theologians, and through the everyday common-sense but seriously conducted moral argument over justice and human rights, or over public service and private obligation.

There is therefore one aspect of an education which takes the teaching of values seriously, namely, attention to the development of *reasonableness* as that is implicit in what I have so far said. The accusation of relativism arises (quite wrongly) from the recognition that there is an inevitable diversity of values – of views about the life worth pursuing – without an agreed procedure for resolving those differences. From that it is falsely argued that the values one holds are 'subjective' or ultimately 'a matter of taste', certainly not a matter of reasonableness. However, such a conclusion is patently false. Through arguing, making sense of competing views, reviewing the evidence, being awakened to alternative ideals, coping with criticism, so does one change *over time* the views that one holds. That change arises through greater clarification, the perception of inconsistencies, the broadening of one's perspective, the greater insight into aspects of human nature, the enrichment of one's awareness of possibilities, and so on. It is part of the deliberative and reflective life seriously engaged in. And it requires time, the opportunity and the encouragement so to reflect and deliberate, without the expectation of reaching conclusions officially approved.

Such a sense of 'reasonableness' would, as I have indicated, draw upon a public tradition of 'reasoning' about such matters as that reflected in literary, artistic and moral traditions. Indeed, the job of the teacher in this, the very core of education, is to mediate those public traditions to the personal deliberations of each and every learner. The good teacher has two major qualities. First, he or she is rooted in an aspect of that public and changing conversation between the generations which has something important to say on matters of human concern; such a teacher has to some measure internalised, and finds enjoyment in, some aspect of that public tradition; he or she wishes to communicate it, to bring others into the conversation. Second, the good teacher also understands the level of aspiration and deliberation of the pupils he or she is responsible for. Education in this respect is essentially a transaction between the teacher, on the one hand, participating in a public though changing tradition of understanding and appreciation, and the learner, on the other, deliberating about conflicting values, struggling for answers to difficult questions.

The key question is: how can we bring together that public world (in literature, in art, in drama, in ritual, etc.), that the teacher is familiar with, and that still private world of the learner as he or she struggles with solutions to personal and social problems, which solutions will finally determine that young person's quality of life?

That attempt to bring together the public and the private, the world of public discourse and the world of personal feelings and understandings, is the story of each person who seriously is engaged in sorting out his or her future. And that quality of 'moral seriousness' – which is potentially there in every learner – should be the focus of all those who take the teaching of values (that is, who take education) seriously. This was explained in a recent paper critical of that growing literature on 'effective schools' which ignores these central questions of education.

> I am not talking about anything esoteric. I am talking about the young person who stops to think about how he should live his life, who commits him or herself to certain people or causes, who refuses to treat others as mere pawns in his or her particular game, who pauses before embarking upon a dodgy enterprise, who is genuinely puzzled by challenges to received assumptions and values, who takes seriously any criticism of standards in behaviour or work, who finds challenging the exploration of what is right or worthwhile in literature or art or science, who cares about the environment and other social and political issues, who does not run away from the deeper questions of meaning and value and purpose. Such a moral perspective is not confined to the most able or the most privileged. And it must not be confused with cleverness or interest in argument. It is a matter of *seriousness* in thinking about what is worth living for, what is worth pursuing in the arts or the leisure time, what relationships are worth entering into, what kinds of activities should be avoided, what obligations are to be considered sacred. What is distinctive of being a person is this capacity for being serious about life, a capacity requiring the application of intelligence, of moral judgement, of reflection

and of sensitivity, which is often fostered by teachers even when much in
the commercial environment militates against it, and even when it finds
no place in the literature of the effective school or of the learning society.
(Pring, 1997)

However, it is precisely this respect for the moral seriousness of young
people and for the development of reasonableness – the deliberation and
reflection over time, in the light of public discourse and evidence – which
is increasingly excluded from the curriculum of schools and which is
largely seen to be indifferent to the so-called 'effective school'. Such is
the need for syllabuses to be covered, for pre-defined attainment levels to
be reached, for achievement in those things which can be easily measured,
for focus upon those skills and knowledge which are supposedly of
economic benefit, that the potential moral seriousness of each learner and
the 'trying to make sense of the world of values one necessarily inhabits
get increasingly neglected. There is little room or time or personal
resources of the teacher left over for that long-term deliberative process,
the ends of which can never be predicted or predetermined. Indeed, the
main victims of the first Dearing review, without argument or explanation,
were the humanities and the arts – the very areas of the curriculum which
provide the *public* grounds for the *intersubjective* exploration which
leads, in different ways, to *personal* resolution.

INSTITUTIONAL VALUES

Teachers cannot pursue these matters alone. They work within institutions
which have their own ethos and agendas, and within constraints of
curriculum and timetable. And these institutions operate within a wider
political framework which increasingly determines the form of discourse
within which values are understood and explored. Let me consider each
of these points in turn – the institutional ethos and the wider political
framework and discourse which affect that ethos.

Institutional ethos

Kohlberg's research into the enhancement of principled reasoning about
moral and social matters – into shifting the quality of thinking from the
egotistical and preconventional mode of reasoning to the more objective
and conventional and then to the more universalistic and principled – was
confronted with the age-old problem of converting thought into
behaviour, principles into practice. His conclusion was that, unless these

principles of fairness and justice, unless the principles of respect for persons, permeate the institution and its community, they will not, however effective the classroom instruction, be internalised within the dispositions of the learners and into their mode of thinking which translates naturally into practice. The work of Power and Reimer (1978) long ago reinforced Kohlberg's conclusion. They noted a developmental sequence in both the normative values within a group and in the sense of community. The general point is that the connection between thought and action depends upon the general atmosphere and expectations of the wider community. How individuals behave will depend upon the values which operate in public life and upon the interaction between the individual and those values within a developed sense of community.

Following this up, Kohlberg (1982) created his Just Community Schools. To quote:

> In summary, the current demand for moral education is a demand that our society becomes more of a just community. If our society is to become a more just community, it needs democratic schools. This was the demand and dream of Dewey. (p. 24)

The idea of 'democratic schools' obviously needs to be treated with care. It does not mean that everything which transpires within them is open to majority vote! Teachers are appointed because they are 'authorities' within their subject area. Schools operate within a framework of laws and public expectation. But what it does signify is a respect – which needs to be translated into the curriculum and into modes of teaching – for the concerns and the beliefs of those who are being taught. It means creating space in which there might be the scope for reflection and deliberation over time. It requires, too, the development of those teaching skills which enable that transaction to take place between the public tradition of knowledge and appreciation, which we have inherited, and the personal worlds of the pupils who are trying to make sense of their lives.

Schools should be the place where that encounter takes place – indeed, is encouraged. But that can only happen where they, and the teachers within them, participate in a wider community, where the relationship between education and values is constantly explored – and where the uncertainties which permeate our exploration of educational aims are respected. The point is that, just as teachers should, especially within the humanities and the arts, encourage the exploration of values without predetermining the conclusions to be reached (they should treat the

seriousness of young people seriously), so too should our political masters
encourage the teachers themselves constantly to explore the aims and
values of education, knowing that no one, certainly not the chief executive
of the Qualifications and Curriculum Authority (QCA), will ever reach a
final set of conclusions.

It is, in this respect, strange how little importance is attached to the arts
and the humanities, so much so that, as I have already mentioned, these
important areas of the curriculum have been made no longer compulsory
after the age of 14. Furthermore, the QCA suggestions for personal,
social, moral and spiritual education (advised, I understand, by a
professional philosopher) pay but lip service to the arts and humanities
(QCA, 1998). And, again, the QCA agenda for citizenship, emphasising
as it does the importance of political literacy, is written as though that
literacy is not to be found within the teaching of history and the social
studies, within the analysis of drama and literature, or within the images
embodied within the arts (Crick Report, 1998; Pring, 1999).

However, as Stenhouse (1975) argued in connection with the
Humanities Curriculum Project, the issues which divide society on the
basis of value (the use of violence, the justice of war, the tolerance of
differences, the acceptance of poverty, sexual relations, respect for
authority, faithfulness to family, loyalty to one's country, obedience to the
law) are also the issues which, in different ways perhaps, are the serious
concern both of the young learner, trying to make sense of his or her
personal life, and of the serious artist or writer, trying to make sense of the
public world of meanings and images. The teaching of both the arts and
the humanities is central and not peripheral to personal, social and moral
development since it puts the individual in touch with the public dialogue
and assists personal efforts to find out and to understand what is valuable
and what is the right course of action. The personal exploration becomes
linked to the longer term and public exploration; it is put in touch with the
resources of poetry and drama, of religious enquiry and of historical
understanding. And this is done within the context of a social group, keen
to understand through discussion, criticism and the study of evidence.

Political framework and form of discourse

This is not easy. Many teachers do in fact participate in a tradition (one
which is regularly and contemptuously dismissed as 'child centred') in
which the concerns and aspirations of the young learners matter. But that
tradition is not easy to maintain when the discourse of education is
dominated more by the utilitarian demands of economic betterment rather

than the moral demands of personal fulfilment. Hence, the low priority given to the arts and the humanities, which have little significance in league tables and judgments about 'effectiveness' and standards. The very language of education – the language of inputs and outputs, of performance indicators and audits, of the delivery of curriculums and of market choice, of schools as businesses and of learners as customers – this very language of institutional and corporate management is an impoverishment of the moral discourse within which education might be seen as that encounter between the young learners and the public traditions in which what is worthwhile rather than useful is openly explored.

This is reflected in the increasing demand to think 'in business terms'. Such thinking requires a clear and unambiguous statement of the product, an empirically sound route to achieving that product, accountability to the stakeholders' for these products and processes involved, measurement of the product reached, an unambiguous statement to the customers about the product, so that they might make a rational choice, and a partnership between stakeholders, customers and producers.

Such a six-point business plan (see Pring, 1999), now permeating the discourse in education, transforms the very institutions of learning, and educational climate, in which the exploration of values, which I have described, is to take place. It is difficult to see how such exploration, the exact outcomes of which cannot be predicted, is compatible with the prespecification of product that the new managers of education think to be necessary. The emphasis on the 'effective school' which measures effectiveness in terms of the most efficient and cost-effective way of generating the product, finds little room for that moral seriousness which requires reflection, the tolerance of criticism, the readiness to think again, the patience for accepting slow and often painful progress.

In effect, such personal exploration and seriousness are too important and personal (albeit participating in a public and social tradition of enquiry) to be subject to the national assessment of progress required of 'the business plan'. To attempt to do so (and yet what else is there for measuring and comparing the products of different schools?) would be to set a range of constraints inimical to that personal growth and a key stage of development.

Moreover, the teachers themselves, in order to develop this moral seriousness in the students and the accompanying dispositions or virtues, must themselves be part of that wider community which is engaged in such exploration of the moral purposes and the aims of education. What sort of life is worth living and preparing the next generation for is a perennial question, never to be fully answered, which underpins such notions as the 'effective school', or the most appropriate system of education, or the choice of schools, or the 'selection from the culture' of what should appear on the school curriculum.

It was with that in mind that Morrell worked so hard to create the kind of forum in which the teachers, participating in a continuing, essentially moral debate, might translate that debate into classroom practice – through reform in the curriculum of the humanities and the rest. For, as he argued:

> our educational crisis is fundamentally part of a general crisis of values. If education, and by implication the curriculum, is not thought of as contributing to a solution of this crisis of values, it can all too easily become an agent of the worst sort of conservatism. (Morrell, 1967, p. 14)

CONCLUSIONS

There is a strange reaction to a national curriculum which, defined in terms of an aggregate of subjects, seems to neglect what now many in authority are saying should be central to education – namely, the teaching of values whether those be moral values, spiritual awareness and sensitivity, or citizenship. For that reason, much guidance is forthcoming to teachers – after firm rejections of relativism. There *is* something to teach.

But much of such guidance fails on three counts.

First, there is quite inadequate analysis of the nature of moral disagreement, the different levels at which that disagreement takes place, and the compatibility of disagreement with reasonableness in tackling disagreement.

Second, much of the advice ignores that central educational concern for personal and moral development, so obvious in many curriculum projects over the years and in the practice of many teachers, but manifest in the teaching of literature, drama, history, social studies and the arts. There is a tradition of humanities teaching which needs to be preserved, but can so easily be neglected through the detailed 'reforms' of the advocates of central control and effective schools.

Third, however, this tradition is ill-at-ease with a shifting form of educational discourse which has little place for the exploration of value, the open endedness of discussion, the acceptance of uncertainty and the tolerance of difference.

REFERENCES

Dearing Report (1994) *The National Curriculum and Its Assessment.* London, SCAA.
Han, C. (1996) 'Education for Citizenship in a Plural Society', PhD thesis, University of Oxford.
Hare, R.M. (1952) *The Language of Morals.* Oxford, Oxford University Press.
Kohlberg, L. (1982) 'Recent Work in Moral Education', in L.O. Ward (ed.), *The Ethical Dimension of the School Curriculum.* Swansea, Pineridge Press.
Morrell, D. (1967) 'Education and Change', The Annual Joseph Payne Memorial Lectures, London, College of Preceptors.
Power, C. and Reimer, J. (1978) 'Moral Atmosphere', in W. Damon (ed.), *New Direction for Child Development and Moral Development.* San Francisco, Jossey-Bass.
Pring, R. (1997) 'Educating Persons', in R. Pring and G. Walford (eds), *Affirming the Comprehensive Ideal.* London, Falmer Press.
Pring, R. (1999) 'Political Education: Relevance of the Humanities', *Oxford Review of Education.*
Qualifications and Curriculum Authority (QCA) (1998) *Education for Citizenship and the Teaching of Democracy in Schools, Initial Report* (Crick Report). London, QCA.
Qualifications and Curriculum Authority (1998) *Promotion of Pupils' Spiritual, Moral, Social and Cultural Development.* London, QCA.
Raths, L.E. (1966) *Values and Teaching.* Wembley, Merrill.
Rawls, J. (1993) *Political Liberalism.* New York, Columbia University Press.
Ross, W.D. (1939) *The Foundation of Ethics.* Oxford, Oxford University Press.
Simon, S.B. (1972) *Values Clarification: A Handbook.* New York, Hart.
Stenhouse, L. (1975) *Authority, Education and Emancipation.* London, Heinemann.
Wilson, J. *et al.* (1967) *An Introduction to Moral Education.* Harmondsworth, Penguin.

Part IV:

An International Perspective on Education in Values

9

CULTURAL VALUES, HUMAN RIGHTS AND RELIGION IN THE CURRICULUM

David Morrison

The power of electronic interlinking, with its ramifications for identity penetration, is universally recognised. Internationalisation in banking and economic realities has, in essence, created a borderless world. The correlation of nation-states with value identity is lessening. For example, my own country, Canada, is referred to as multicultural, with a major segment having an identifiable separatist movement. As a foreigner in the United Kingdom, I do not recognise a strong particular British *culture*, but when pressed can identify Scottish, Welsh, Irish, Celtic, English (with its sub-sets), almost all of which contain separatist movements too. What we are recognising is a pressure to break down barriers, held in tension with the need to create new identities. Within this changing framework, we look for values. Where are they to be found – in the tradition of religions, of nation-states, of ethnic homogeneity? Where do they prevail in relation to cultures and in the new international framework?

Values do not exist in a void. They give meaning to the culture and society in which they are expressed. In turn, culture and society provide the power determinant of what shall be *valued*. 'Cultural' values can be universal but are applied in particular situations. Even if we are able to agree on what universals may be considered as values to be protected, taught and expounded, we can appreciate that their absorption into the social fabric will be influenced by the divisions which exist in any community. Theoretically, the democratic process keeps these diversities in tension.[1] For our purpose, it will be important to determine if there is a role for agreed-upon standards in upholding, teaching and promoting values as embodied in international human-rights instruments.

Culture may be seen as the sum of human practices and experiences that not only reflect reality in some way but that also construct reality and give it meaning. So it is that culture is appreciated from both the 'inside' and the 'outside', with vastly different interpretations. What is significant is the influence of human-rights goals throughout each of these 'cultures', locally as well as globally. Another word for goal is the term *value*, which represents what people consider important in life.

> They are ideas about what is good, worth having, and worth trying to achieve. The Universal Declaration represents a set of values that the members nations of the General Assembly have pledged themselves to try to attain. (Fraenkel, 1975, p.75)

There is little doubt that specific cultural values do come into conflict with one another, but we have reached a stage where it is possible to at least affirm a creed of commitment to individual worth and human dignity. It is in the sub-sets of culture and society where there has been most human rights' activity, such as against racism, for women's rights, for children, for the physically and mentally challenged and so on. Many of these have a history before current emphases which now continue to be galvanised. This has long been true in the women's movement which has a sterling history, yet a long journey to travel.

Cultural values and human rights combine the old and new, moral demands and legal claims. The Harvard ethicist Arthur Dyck points out that moral bonds provide a basis for there being rights and for making it both possible and meaningful to claim them, if and when that becomes necessary. He suggests that:

> in a relatively well-ordered community in which these moral bonds are largely strong and intact, rights are expectations, mostly below the threshold of awareness, that individuals and groups will not be destructive of existing moral bonds. If and when, however, given moral bonds are threatened or destroyed, rights may take the form of claims. These claims may be solely moral or both moral and legal. (Dyck, 1994, p. 145)

The world-wide tendency to democracy assumes that societies are open and striving to achieve greater levels of equality. From this perspective, values are based in all sectors of society: ethnic and religious; political and economic; educational – through schools and universities, and their curricula. The need to balance a search for values within a democratic society is held in tension with continuing demands by specific groups to have their separate identities, rights and participation levels fully recognised (Taylor, 1992). Part of a demand for recognition by religious and ethnic minorities, women, blacks and coloured, young and ageing, arises from the fact that they know and feel that they are treated unequally. A strand of opinion suggests that this reflects a need for an acknowledgment of these various identities – and a development of educative strategies which can be implemented into curricula and which respect religious and social distinctions. *Do universally accepted human rights standards constitute a valid education model and challenge for a broader ethic of values in socially diverse cultures?*

CONFLICT AND DIALOGUE

If ever there has been a prolonged search for resolution to human behaviour, it has been in the arena of conflict – be it driven by the *angst* of a moral imperative searching for values or a religious and esoteric response to *hubris*. Compounded over time, economic, social and cultural injustice becomes the primary cause of perpetuating prejudice, racism and even violent attitudes leading to conflicts such as wars, long after reasons of precipitating (e.g. religious) factors have ceased to be prominent.

There needs to be room within the democratic framework for an increase in dialogue as an attempt to ensure that the values we share as human beings individually and at a universal level are based on genuine principles. One of the hallmarks of prejudicial practices is a behaviour based solely on feelings. Surely an adequate understanding of a society must originate from basic commitments, from values, not from attitudes. The necessity of dialogue is important because of the emergence of unattractive alternatives. Paulo Freire (1994) reminds us of the creative moment of differences:

> We definitely need the virtue of tolerance, which is still scarce among us; we are almost always intolerant. For example, when someone thinks differently than we do, we state that person is wrong. It is terrible to discover these things! We must not engage in controversy, however, we must dialogue. Instead of engaging in controversy about the difference, we must hold a dialogue about the difference. (p. 91)

In a word, what is a contemporary ethical position in the search for authentic values? Cultural organisations – ethnic, social, religious and humanistic – join other parts of society and generally affirm the principles of human rights as found in the various international instruments. The eminent theologian Hans Küng (1991), for one, outlines his major project for encouraging an ethical quest. His conclusion is this:

> The programme which guides us and which comes together as one may be summed up once again in three basic statements: no human life together without a world ethic for the nations; no peace among the nations without peace among the religions; no peace among the religions without dialogue among the religions. (p. 138)

Küng, like many others, has come face to face with the absence of a value system as a *modus* for the present world. The assertions of short-term and private gains taking precedent over long-term public interest are eroding social mores and cultural standards.

SECULAR AND RELIGIOUS FREEDOM

Once again, there can be no competing claim for religious or social rights unless they are subordinate to the rights of the human race (and the environment) to live and survive. The Dalai Lama, leader of the Tibetan Buddhists, speaking to representatives of the Buddhist, Christian, Jewish, Muslim, Sikh and other religions (in Ottawa, Canada), said that:

> we have to think seriously about closer relations between various spiritual traditions. Each religion has the potential to help humanity, so that's a sufficient reason to come together and work together. All of the different religious faiths, despite their philosophical differences, have a similar objective. Every religion emphasizes human improvement, love respect for others, sharing other peoples' suffering. On these lines every religion has more or less the same viewpoint and the same goal. Those faiths which emphasize Almighty God and faith in and love of God have as their purpose the fulfilment of God's intentions. Seeing us all as creations of and followers of one God, they teach that we should cherish and help each other. The very purpose of faithful belief in God is to accomplish His wishes, the essence of which is to cherish, respect, love, and give service to our fellow humans. (in Griffiths, 1990, p. 163)

While values are supported in the quest for both religious and secular freedom, most remarkably through international and regional human rights instruments, a complementary response is critical. Leadership from religions for the promotion and implementation of all fundamental human rights and freedoms would be revolutionary in terms of human dignity. An early intellectual, political and pedagogical pursuit of this goal by religious bodies and scholars would assure that their particular legal/doctrinal (human rights) structures reflect or at least approximate the universally accepted standards of behaviour. It has begun. In the Christian Churches, especially in the northern hemisphere and Latin America, there are several recent and vigorous movements for the implementation of charters of rights for the churches and for church members, to realise democracy and human rights within the Church (see Human Rights Unit, 1991). The application of human-rights principles within the major world religions will go a long way towards the enhancing of human dignity – in concert with nation-states which already have approved the human-rights principles. This concentrism of interests has forced the religious factor to be cognizant of 'secular' value standards. David Little (1988) is correct when he says that the different religions of the world no doubt respond differently to common points of orientation and common problems, and to an important extent those differences constitute crucial divergences and areas of contention among them. But through human rights values, 'members of the world's religions are all potentially partners in a grand intercultural "multilogue" to be organised around the shared points of reference' (p. 27). Excepting the fundamentalist margins, the creative edge of growth in humanistic/secular values has had a positive effect on the scholastic and popular presentation of religious formulations and identities.

Education is not value free, claiming to be based on democratic principles and on human rights which purport to be opposed to racism and fascism and aiming, at least officially, at mutual understanding. Educators would be aware of the pedagogical function of education and the root values on which education is based. Therefore, it is important to define basic ethical and cultural values which can be mediated with parents and students, a process which in itself ought to promote mutual understanding. Since education is usually provided by the state or state sanction, institutionalised education belongs to the broader catchment. Is religion in a secular society to be relegated to the private domain when we discuss values and curriculum? This division itself is problematic in a multicultural society. That is one reason we are here. *Is it possible that values would mutually penetrate each cultural domain through human rights curricula?*

Many governments have agreed to implement the provisions of existing international human-rights instruments as well as modify their own domestic legislative provisions to correspond to these changes. These reflect an awareness of change in basic values. Where there is the educational and political will, it is feasible to develop various levels of human-rights education. The thrust is simply to appreciate what has been agreed upon already – the standards of the major human-rights instruments and the obligation from all governments that those principles be disseminated as widely as possible. Moreover, considerable curriculum has already been developed.

Pedagogical goals are aimed at the development of the attitudes and behaviour of individuals based on an awareness of values (Haydon, 1987). Let us use one example. Women in society and particularly in religion occupy a sensitive place. There is a growing body of research and reflection on women in society and on women in religion. Models of feminist theology have been forwarded by various scholars. More and more female Islamic scholars join the ranks of Christian feminists who can assist the broader society on the role of women and human-rights education. Research is now creating models required to combat the discrimination and intolerance against women existing in all religions. This effort will also impact in the field of international law and the progress of economic and cultural development, that is econometric studies have made it clear that female education rates have a very significant effect on development. Where religions do not encourage higher educational attainment for females, there is a real sense in which religious influence thus contributes to higher infant mortality, lower health levels for children and prevents social and economic development not only for the present but for future generations. As one senior World Bank official has reminded us: 'Just imagine how much better off the world would be today if major investments in increasing female education had been made a generation ago' (Husain, 1993).

TOLERATION AND ACCEPTANCE

Ethnic and religious toleration continues to be a delicate issue of our times. At the international level, there is a growing sensitivity to changing patterns of acceptable behaviours. The topic belongs front and centre in any contemporary consideration of values and conflict resolution. Everyday we see individuals crushed by society. Rarely is society torn apart by the exercise of individual human rights; instead social disorder and decay are usually associated with the violation of individual human rights by the state or some organised segment of society. Human rights are a rare and valuable constitutional, intellectual and moral resource, in the struggle to correct the balance of power between society (and the state) and the individual. Unless we preserve their distinctive character, including standing firm on their character as individual rights, a positive role in the struggle for human dignity would be seriously, perhaps even fatally, compromised (Donnelly, 1990).

The international community of scholars is acutely aware of the need for multicultural and multireligious cooperation and indeed, mutual acceptance. The search for behaviour values which reflect the fact of a shared sense of human dignity can be found in human rights. The motif of acceptance goes well beyond any attempt at 'mere tolerance', which can assume some rather imperialistic forms. Even when taught, attitudes to the neighbour as 'other' can be of various types: exclusivism, which sees one's identity group (race, culture, religion) as superior and the other as 'acceptable' but certainly inferior; inclusivism, which recognises the other as having value and worth, because the self or group accepts it but still sees the neighbour as stranger and inferior; and equality, which sees the other with a full acceptance and respect. A behaviour which withholds this equality and respect is not full tolerance. It is inadequate and falls short of both the idea of dignity and of the demands of human rights ... and without a substantive tolerance of values held in social diversity, there is no chance for a lessening of conflict.

Thinking of human rights as a way of developing values which can be transmitted through education should make educators comfortable with the idea of generating values from rights in a concrete manner, thus entering the realm where positive education can deal with concepts such as human dignity. The concept of human dignity has a broad acceptability through usage and grounding in the Universal Declaration, although there is room for philosophical and cultural debate as to its *precise* meaning. A strong sense that this notion can be seen to underlie any religious or secular formulation is now admissible. Not only is human dignity the bonding cornerstone of the various human rights, it is the essential quality of becoming fully human. Any act or tendency which violates the possibility of actualising human dignity becomes an illicit process overthrowing a potential union of persons with their culture and with the environment. Religions can play a part in seeking a solution to the current problem of diminished values by recognising 'human dignity' through accepted human rights principles. 'To put it bluntly: no regressive or repressive religion – whether Christian, Islamic, Jewish or of whatever provenance – has a long-term future' (Küng, 1991, p. 23).

Education through human-rights instruments is appropriate because the values embodied therein have legal, political and moral force. The notion of human dignity is fundamental to them all and underscores the principles of toleration and acceptance for all nations of the human family.

RESPECT AND VALUES

The relations between people and culture pose problems because cultural diversity raises complex issues. These too can only be resolved if respect for cultural distinctions is a shared basic value. The role of (intercultural) education in protecting this fundamental value has a great significance. The language of human rights offers a vehicle for an understanding of the way in which communities can express a belief about what is sacred or special in human relations. At the same time, there are competing views of humanity which can undercut the sense of dignity by making conflicting claims on how civilisation will be shaped.

Common basic values are marred by the inequalities which exist in society and in the domination or subordination of groups. In many societies, cultural relationships are governed or influenced by the ethnic or the religious factor. This can lead to the rise of both religious and secular counterforces which include: ethnocentrism, racism and fascism; violence and vandalism; rampant consumerism and pollution. Children bring a range of cultural frameworks into the picture. Development of bridges to promote genuinely democratic values in pluralistic contexts requires a sophisticated and rich vocabulary. As Tapio Poulmatka (1990) suggests:

> The beginning of value education includes teaching a rich vocabulary of values and helping the child to gradually relate his (her) own value cognition to value terms and in this way making him more conscious of his ability to recognize values and to state them in words. (p. 11)

The modern value dilemmas (in what has been described as the 'moronic inferno') do have an exceedingly dangerous manifestation with the rise of narrow nationalism, chauvinism, fanaticism, neo-fascism, racism and sexism. In a period when alienation and cynicism are rife, the role of formal education as utilitarian is not enough. Dudley Plunkett argues for a spiritual education in which the mind, the heart and the spirit would engage with reason, intuition and faith. In moving away from an instrumentalist approach to an education of the child, Plunkett (1990) advocates looking at a child holistically: 'Xenophobia can be finally rooted out only when xenophobes undergo moral and spiritual change.' A collective approach to the value issue may allow the school to develop a strategy to deal with these complex matters. These complex behaviours are confronted through a myriad of human-rights instruments. There do exist commentaries and reflections on human rights from various religious and ideological points of view – Islam, Buddhism, Hinduism, Christianity, Humanism and so on. Unfortunately, these are not widely disseminated.

Another real issue is how schools can deal with subliminal attitudes which may be narrow and particularistic, even prejudicial. Many young people find themselves disempowered. They have no control of their own lives. They have lost confidence in the 'democratic state'. The lack of identification with any democratic process is significant. Human-rights education allows participation in the democratic process. The role of the school in teaching human-rights education can ensure that all children are able to participate within the framework of universally accepted standards of behaviour which cross secular and religious cultures.

CONCLUSION

As nation-states have continued to build human rights principles into their constitutions and laws in order to give a goal for high ethical values, self-interest groups (such as religions) may be fast evolving to the stage when they are compelled to subject themselves to the notion of value ethics derived from human dignity as exemplified by international human rights standards. Why? Their interest in any absolutist claims will give way to co-operative affirmations *if they are interested in the survival of humanity.*

Values such as non-discrimination and democratic deliberation are required to offer all threatened and minority groups (especially racial, ethnic and religious minorities) substantive protection. These values are found in most international and regional human-rights (legal) documents. These standards or values may serve as points of dialogue and as teaching tools for educators. Education entitles students to have an opportunity to receive a solid base in the appreciation of cultural values such as respect, equality and toleration. Most of all, values refer to relations – between persons and others, culture and nature. The status of belief systems in all societies, no matter how diverse, affect these three relationships. Once again, we note that cultural relativism is the pressure point for value determination. The educator Douglas Sloan (1980) pointed this out:

> For a great many people, values derive from a religious commitment. That commitment may throw people into conflict with the dominant values of

a society or it may reinforce those values. It is hard to imagine any serious religious commitment that does not shape the values of its adherents. On the other hand, in an increasingly secularized world, it becomes obvious that many people maintain value-laden commitments without participation in formal religious organizations. The change from many past cultural situations is obvious … But for most people, even in secularized cultures, profound loyalties and identities are related in some way to a concrete history and to cultic expression. (p. 117)

This chapter has accentuated the idea that human rights can be the connection between belief systems and cultures in the search for an enunciation of societal values. An ingredient of full toleration is the ability to accept the separateness of the other while striving for a reunion of diversities: a hallmark of democracy.

As educationalists and others attempt to overcome potential conflict through sustaining a democratic union of many divergencies, we have suggested that human-rights education offers an approach to values in which communities can talk about that which is sacred or special in human relations.

Values, emanating from the state or from differing belief systems and religions, stand front and foremost in the attempt to build bridges of understanding between and among people of various cultures. Human rights (including the rights of the child) serve as a structure which can project a positive affirmation to the identity of groups and peoples who are lost as pawns in the disparities of society. The majority of these are young persons.

NOTES

1. I am indebted to Dr Jagdish Gundara of the Institute of Education's International Centre for Intercultural Studies with whom a joint paper was prepared for the Institute of Commonwealth Studies on 'Values and Social Diversity: Human Rights and the Religious Factor'. Some of those thoughts appear in this chapter.

REFERENCES

Dalai Lama (1990) '"Religious Harmony" and extracts from The Bodhgaya Interviews', in P. J. Griffiths, *Christianity Through Non-Christian Eyes*. New York, Orbis Books.
Donnelly, J. (1990), 'Human Rights, Individual Rights and Collective Rights', in J. Bergen *et al.* (eds), *Human Rights in a Pluralist World: Individuals and Collectivities*. Netherlands Commission for UNESCO, London, Meckler.

Dyck, A. J. (1994) *Rethinking Rights and Responsibilities: The Moral Bonds of Community*. Cleveland, The Pilgrim Press.

Fraenkel, J. R. (1975) *The Struggle for Human Rights: A Question of Values*. New York, Random House.

Freire, P. (1994) *Paulo Freire on Higher Education: A Dialogue at the National University of Mexico*. Albany, State University of New York Press.

Haydon, G. (1987) 'Towards a Framework of Commonly Accepted Values', in G. Haydon *et al.*, *Education for a Plural Society*. London, Institute of Education, University of London.

Human Rights Unit (1991) *Understanding the Issues: A Study of Human Rights Principles Proposed for the Anglican Church of Canada*. Toronto, Anglican Church of Canada.

Husain, T. (1993). *Keynote Address to the International Conference of the Association of Canadian County Colleges*. Ottawa.

Küng, H. (1991). *Global Responsibility: In Search of a New World Ethic*. London, SCM Press.

Little, D. (1988) *Human Rights and the Conflict of Cultures*. Columbia, University of South Carolina Press.

Plunkett, D. (1990), *Secular and Spiritual Values: Ground for Hope in Education*. London, Routledge.

Poulmatka, T. (1990) *Pluralism and Education in Values*. Helsinki, University of Helsinki Research Bulletin.

Sloan, D. (ed.) (1980) *Education and Values*. New York, Teachers College Press.

Taylor, C. (1992) *Multiculturalism and The Politics of Recognition*. Princeton, NJ, Princeton University Press.

10

NEW WINE IN RENEWED WINESKINS: A JESUIT SCHOOL NOW

Paddy Walsh

THE JESUIT TRADITION

Jesuit schools have been a near constant since the foundation of the Jesuits in the Catholic Counter-Reformation of the sixteenth century. St Ignatius personally approved the foundation of 40 schools, which must have absorbed a significant proportion of the fewer than 1,000 Jesuits at the time of his death in 1556. Within a further 40 years the number of schools had reached a remarkable 245, by no means all in Europe. Schools and colleges together numbered 845 in 1773, the year in which this network was largely destroyed by the Papal suppression of the Jesuits. Undaunted, Jesuits started over again on their educational mission when another Pope restored them to existence in 1814. By 1987 their involvement extended to some 2,000 educational institutions providing education for 1,500,000 young people and adults in 56 countries (ICJE, 1987, *Characteristics*, paras. 189,194,196).

This chapter first identifies and discusses key elements in the radical renewal of Jesuit educational philosophy since the Second Vatican Council. It then presents a case study of St Simon's, a Jesuit, college-preparatory, day high school (14–18) for boys in a north-eastern American city – one of 46 Jesuit high schools in the USA. St Simon's was chosen, on the recommendation of a trusted educationist, as an example of a school taking its Jesuit commitment imaginatively and seriously – and thus offering an opportunity to study the re-thought Jesuit philosophy in action. The study presented here is both interim – more refined methods of data analysis are still to be attempted – and partial – focusing in particular on aspects of the school's spiritual and moral education.[1]

The review of Jesuit philosophy relies on a convenient collection of 14 official and quasi-official documents, from the period between 1970 and 1993, compiled by the Jesuit Secondary Education Association of America (Meirose, 1994). It draws especially on two of the most seminal and international of these documents. *Man for Others* is a 1974 address to a Congress of European Jesuit Alumni by Pedro Arrupe (the charismatic leader, or 'General', of the Jesuits for most of the period under review), which rapidly became part of the canon of modern Jesuit thinking on education and is frequently echoed in later documents. *Go Forth to Teach: The Characteristics of Jesuit Education* (*Characteristics*), is a 40 page mission-cum-policy handbook published in 1987 by The International Commission on the Apostolate of Jesuit Education after 'four years of meetings and international consultations' (para. 6). It is addressed to 'teachers, administrators, parents and governing bodies' in Jesuit schools and colleges, and offers 'a common vision and a common sense of purpose ... against which we measure ourselves' (para. 11).

The main part of the fieldwork was conducted in December 1995 and the methods used included analysis of school documents, observation of some classes and school activities, semi-structured interviews of 12 key staff members and a student questionnaire. The interviewees, nine lay-persons and three Jesuits, were selected for me by the Principal to meet specified broad criteria, and in particular for their engagement with the Jesuit character of the school – about which they were without exception highly articulate. The hour-long student questionnaire contained 170 items focusing, first, on the respondents' perceptions of the school and its curriculum and, second, on their own values, goals, beliefs, faith, religious practices and religious development, and was administered to a reasonably random sample of 47 'senior' (final year) students – what might be called 'the exit poll' approach. It was a slimmed-down version of the instrument devised by Flynn for his survey of Catholic school leavers in 50 New South Wales schools (Flynn, 1993). I shall make occasional comparisons with Flynn's findings.

Renewal of Jesuit Education since Vatican 2

Starting in 1966 and still continuing, this has been a characteristically thorough, and indeed radical, affair in at least many parts of the Jesuit world (including America), conducted with one eye on Ignatius and the other on the circumstances of modernity, and with Arrupe as the original moving spirit. I shall briefly consider the three most striking developments to have emerged at the theoretical level.

The call to justice

Jesuit schools, famously, have aimed at training leaders who would assume responsible positions in society and there exercise a positive influence on others. The word 'elitism' comes to many people's minds and this association has caused modern Jesuits some embarrassment. 'A propose', it is remarked in *Characteristics*.

> This objective has, at times, led to excesses which call for correction. Whatever the concept may have meant in the past, the goal of Jesuit education in today's understanding of the Ignation world-view is not to prepare a socio-economic elite, but rather to educate leaders in service. The Jesuit school, therefore, will help students to develop the qualities of mind and heart that will enable them – in whatever station they assume in life – to work with others for the good of all in the service of the Kingdom of God. (ICJE, 1987, para. 146)

Of course, this may be thought to rely on a distinction between acceptable and unacceptable forms of elitism. Leadership is still envisaged, even if now it is a leadership in service, 'working with others for the good of all'.

Be that as it may, however, the shift in emphasis is seen as profoundly consequential:

> Today our prime educational objective must be to form men-for-others[2] ... men who cannot even conceive of love of God which does not include love for the least of their neighbours; men completely convinced that love of God which does not issue in justice for men is a farce. (*Men for Others*, Meirose, 1994, p. 32)

In choosing to address this challenge to alumni Arrupe was, one supposes, both sensible, considering the influence of alumni on Jesuit schools, and brave. He can appeal to their Jesuit heritage of openness to new challenges and willingness to undergo conversion, but he is absolutely clear that this challenge is new.

> Have we Jesuits educated you for justice ?.... No, we have not. If the terms 'justice' and 'education for justice' carry all the depth of meaning which the Church gives them today, we have not educated you for justice. (ibid.)

The novelty, as implied here, is not a specifically Jesuit inspiration. Arrupe roots it tellingly in the teachings of Vatican 2, certain encyclicals of Paul VI and, in particular, in the statement on *Justice in the World* of the 1971 Synod of Bishops, from which he quotes:

Action on behalf of justice and participation in the transformation of the world fully appear to us as a constitutive dimension of the preaching of the Gospel …We cannot, then, separate action for justice and liberation from oppression from the proclamation of the Word of God. (ibid. p. 34)

It is not the whole of the Church's mission but it is 'a constitutive dimension'. And for all its congruity with Biblical tradition, this challenge is in a real sense new for the Church too. It is not 'a mere repetition of what the Church has traditionally taught' and 'not a refinement of doctrine at the level of abstract theory' but

an imperious call of the living God asking his Church and all men of good will to adopt certain attitudes and undertake certain types of action which will enable them effectively to come to the aid of mankind oppressed and in agony. (ibid. p. 33)

This call to a justice, said to be in practice identical with charity, is seen as involving, first, a basic attitude of respect for all men, second, a firm resolve never to profit from, or allow ourselves to be suborned by, positions of privilege and, third, an attitude not simply of refusal of injustice but of counter-attack against injustice. It is further analysed as intrinsically social, involving not just an individualist personal conversion but structural reform and a new social asceticism and spirituality. The theological concept of 'concupiscence' and the Biblical concept of 'the world' are invoked to expose, respectively, the continued domination of the effects of sin over the 'peripheries' of Christians who are already converted in their hearts and the objectification of those effects in our social, economic and commercial systems. Arrupe (who presided over the major Jesuit contribution to liberation theology in Latin and Central America) adds that we need secular instruments of analysis and action if we are to

go to a map of the world and point out the critical points – geographical, sociological, cultural – where sin and justice find their lodgement

though we must remember that such instruments are imperfect tools, a mixture of good and evil in their origins, which must be put in their relative, not absolute, place.

The application of these principles to school-age students is taken up in *Characteristics*. This handbook speaks of asking students for an active commitment to the struggle for a more human world and a community of love; of an education for justice that joins adequate knowledge to rigorous and critical thinking; of the treatment of justice issues across the curriculum and a critical analysis of society adapted to the age level of the students; of school self-evaluation and structural changes in school policies and practices to bear counterwitness to the values of a consumer society; of actual student contact with the world of injustice to give an experiential base to their reflections on society; of talents as gifts to be developed, with the help of God, for the good of the human community; of the attitude of mind that sees service of others as more self-fulfilling than success or prosperity; of the poor forming the context of Jesuit education, both in the sense that poor students are admitted to it and in the sense that it should promote a special concern for those men and women who are without the means to live in human dignity; of opportunities for students to have contact with the poor and to serve them joined to reflective analysis of the causes of poverty; and of the pursuit of academic excellence being appropriate in a Jesuit school only within the larger context of human excellence (ICJE, 1987, *Characteristics*, paras. 74–92). Cumulatively, there can be no doubt that these prescriptions make a very powerful statement.

Making Ignation spirituality available to curriculum, pedagogy and ethos

Another aspect of the image of Jesuit schools has been their reputation for thoroughness in both academic and personal formation. Hamilton (1989, 1990) credits Jesuits and Calvinists jointly with the dissemination, if not the invention, of that icon of modernity, the planned, methodically staged, age-related curriculum. Ignatius was indeed seriously committed to educational planning. In his own education as a mature student, he experienced, first, the general lack of planning of the times and, then over seven years, the relatively careful methods of the University of Paris. In adapting the latter for school use, Ignatius was acting out a critical reflection on his own experience. This reflectiveness was soon to be a basic principle of the *Ratio Studiorum*, which evolved through several editions in the generation after his death. It was also a bridge between the humanities pedagogy of Ignatius' schools and his almost equally famous retreat programme, the *Spiritual Exercises*. Perhaps surprisingly, however, it seems that the widening and formal opening of this bridge between spirituality and education in Jesuit schools has had to wait upon the present renewal of Jesuit philosophy.

Already in 1970, the Jesuit Secondary Schools' Commission envisaged translating into educational practices many of the basic principles of the Ignation Spiritual Exercises. The *contemplatio ad amorem*, for instance, by which Jesuits themselves learn to perceive God in nature and human history, would become the educational objective of developing in students a sense of awe and appreciation before the aspects of the world which they encountered in their studies.[3] And pedagogies might be developed for facilitating knowledge by a kind of empathic identification as well as by logical analysis. Ignation 'indifference' or 'detachment' would translate into class examinations of such things as common kinds of prejudice and bigotry and the underlying causes of violence. Ignation meditations on the 'Two Standards and the Kingdom' could entail communicating to students the full human and cosmic drama of our individual and communal histories. Extending to students the Jesuit self-image of 'contemplatives in action' and people committed to the *magis*, the always greater good, suggests a picture of school graduates as simultaneously dreamers and people who take realistic stands to realise their dreams, because their education has deeply affected those basic perceptual structures by which they view themselves and their world. (Meirose, 1994, pp. 1–5) These are ideas which were then confidently and practically re-elaborated in the 1987 *Characteristics* and in the 1993 *Ignation Pedagogy: A Practical Approach* (Meirose, 1994, section 14).

LAY-JESUIT COLLABORATION

The Jesuit Secondary Schools Commission also suggested in 1970:

> If the faculty at a Jesuit school are men and women whose lives are inspired by the Ignation vision, then the question about the percentage of Jesuits on the faculty is not an overriding issue. It is more a question of the quality of the lives of all the faculty, both Jesuit and lay. (Meirose, 1994, p. 2)

This reflected, at once, the greatly reduced density of Jesuits in their schools, the coming age of the laity in the Catholic Church, and the authors' optimism about the prospects of communicating the Ignation spirit and vision to lay members of staff, in particular through the use of the Spiritual Exercises (originally devised at a time when Ignatius himself was a layman). By 1987, *Characteristics* can speak of this collaboration as a more or less established fact; of a sharing of vision, purpose and apostolic effort between Jesuit and lay staff; of regular communication between them at personal, professional and religious levels; and of lay

Directors or Principals of Jesuit schools (*Characteristics*, paras. 118–23). In fact the achievement of this collaborative ideal varies around the Jesuit world, but it is a marked feature of the case-study school – under its first-ever (and remarkably young) lay Principal.

It remains to remark on the processes by which these developments have been, and are being, disseminated through the Jesuit school network. In North America, these include consultation on a spectacular scale, a standard of documentation that threatens to bewitch the researcher, the creation of standing advisory offices, regular regional conferences, intensive programmes for the induction of new teachers and for inservice education at both school and regional levels, and, as we shall see at St Simon's, a wide range of variations and adaptations of the Spiritual Exercises for the spiritual training of both faculty and students. The external observer could hardly fail to be impressed by the apparent dynamism of it all. But what would it look like on the ground?

<h2 style="text-align:center">ST SIMON'S: BASIC INFORMATION</h2>

The school is situated in a largely working-class and quite strongly 'ethnic' area. It is over a century old and many of its parents and faculty are alumni – including its Principal. It enrolls 800+ boys in four cohorts from 'freshmen' to 'seniors', of whom, at present, some 40 per cent are non-white and 15 per cent are non-Catholic. The degree of family stability is high – the proportion of divorced or separated parents is estimated at around 10 per cent. Its mainly catholic faculty numbers 65, including 15 Jesuits (many part-time), and there are also eight counsellors and six administrators. Salaries are above average for American Catholic schools, but significantly lower than in either non-Catholic independent schools or public schools (there being no public subsidy to church schools in the USA). Staff generally feel themselves compensated both by their identification with the school's religious and social mission and by the relative keenness of the students. The curriculum includes English, Mathematics, Science, Computer Science, Theology/Religion, Classical Language, Modern Language, History/Social studies, Fine Arts/Music, Physical Education and electives, of which some, e.g. Holocaust Studies, are interdisciplinary. The school is academically selective (though much less so than an English grammar school), continuation depends on not failing in more than two subjects in any year, and virtually all its graduates go on to four-year college programmes. Like all Catholic schools in the USA it is fee-paying. Its cost of around $5,000 a year in 1995–6 compared with an average of about $3,000 for diocesan High Schools and $10–12,000 for non-Catholic independent schools – since its achievement levels compare rather more with the latter than the former it is perceived as 'good value'. Though over half of the present parents have a third-level degree or diploma, the proportion of blue-collar families is thought to be high. Over 30 per cent of its students have up to a third of their fees remitted for hardship reasons, there are lots of IOUs at the end of the year; for many parents the fees mean second or even third jobs, and the case for more remittance of fees to more families is acknowledged – if only it could be afforded. Fund-raising and protecting and increasing the school's endowment are seen as priorities, and are a particular concern of the Jesuit President of the school. The school also identifies an increase in black enrolment as a priority. In general, the school is unapologetic about being academically selective to a degree – other than being concerned to reduce the rate of transfer of students to academically easier schools – while it works energetically to minimise the social selectivity that the requirement of fees forces upon it. But further consideration of these selectivities is beyond the scope of this chapter.

RELIGIOUS EDUCATION: A 'JUNIOR' RELIGION CLASS

The teacher of this class of 17-year-olds is Tom, a young layman from California. Assignments are being returned as I walked in, with much praise and encouragement and reminders to see him individually about their work in their free periods during the week. Sheets for the next assignment are handed out – the topic will be 'Getting Real about Sex'. Then the class proceeds to the day's main topic, begun in the previous religion lesson. It is the ordination of women, with some reference to the statement Rome had issued a few weeks previously, to the effect that the Pope's known and stated viewpoint on this issue was infallible – maybe! The ensuing discussion of pros and cons is judicious and impressive. The students are reminded of a distinction drawn in the previous lesson between 'big T', Tradition in theology and church life, and 'small t', traditions. How might we know if the all-male clergy is 'big T' or 'small t' tradition? If it implies that women are unequal to men, less than fully human in any way, then it contradicts 'big T' Tradition. But are we sure that it implies that? And what about the claim that the Pope's explicit teachings on this may be infallible? What are the criteria of infallibility in a church teaching? What does the relevant Vatican 2 document say they are? Now think through whether or not the Pope's statement meets them.

As the class draws to its end, Tom tells them: it's going to be your generation that decides this, so get ready for it. What can they do to decide on what is right and work for what is right? They can use inclusive language, support campaigns for women … but, most important, they can *treat* women as equals, 'starting at 3 pm today'.

The general approach had been intellectual and textual – not 'what do you feel?' but 'what are the stated criteria?' – and indeed theological (the catholic concepts of Tradition and Infallibility were invoked and interrogated). Yet this was a liberal and critical intellectualism – they would have to make up their minds about the matter in hand at an appropriate time. At interview Tom remarked that they didn't have apologetics as such but dealt with 'truth questions' in the following broad way: 'take the teaching of Jesus, or the Church – How does it relate to your experience? Now,what do you think about its truth and validity?' This seemed thoroughly Ignatian to Tom.

But the approach was also practical and pastoral. The Church is theirs; they will have the major responsibility for shaping it – thus for deciding on women's ordination – and the practical implications of that start 'from 3 pm today'. Asked for his sense of a theological literacy for graduands, Tom would spontaneously mention knowing the stories (being able to read the Bible literally and symbolically as appropriate), knowing what the church is called to be and to become; and knowing that faith led to action and that this action would include questioning how society is.[4] All the Religious faculty I interviewed agreed that their role was both academic and pastoral. They were themselves academically powerful – all had Masters' degrees in theology – and they aimed at theological literacy in their students, but they were also clear that they were in the business of 'formation', and more directly in that frontline than colleagues from other fields (who also, however, agreed they were in formation).

Thus there was no evidence among them of a strong form of the distinction, common in Britain, between religious education and religious nurture. Rather, they seemed to take a different approach to the point of that distinction by placing a marked emphasis on the students' freedom. The Principal remarked in my opening interview:

> kids here are very comfortable exploring their own spiritual route.

This is borne out in the questionnaire responses of the sample of senior students. Massively in favour of respect for the environment and respect for people whatever their race, nationality or religion, and strongly against stealing small items from large department stores, they are anything but pushovers when it comes to more specifically catholic moral teachings (though, as we shall see later, they are more orthodox in matters of 'faith'.) Thus, they are hugely supportive of the unmarried who live together, largely unconvinced by the Church's official teaching on birth control, divided on abortion, and inclined to favour euthanasia. Though the Church is very important for half of the sample and unimportant for only a quarter, only 11 per cent try to follow the catholic way of life unquestioningly, only 28 per cent have not rejected aspects of the Church's teaching in which they once believed, and two-thirds approved the proposition that they had developed their own way of relating to God apart from the Church. Most also claimed that they are coming to believe because of their own conviction rather than the beliefs of others. All this (which is very similar to what Flynn found in his more general study) could be read as evidence either of an independence of mind that is encouraged by the school or of the power of American public opinion. In fact, it probably reflects a combination of both.

There is some ambivalence in the sample's perceptions of RE. Strongly appreciative of the programmes and teaching – 74 per cent were enjoying their final-year RE classes (Flynn 50 per cent) – and of a range of more specific features like the coverage of Catholic teachings and contemporary moral issues and the space provided for discussion, convinced (though by a smaller majority) of the value of RE, the sample yet strongly inclines to the view that RE is not taken seriously by students. For many of these final-year students, however, this is probably a matter of its relative unimportance in gaining desirable college places. That they also generally identify RE as a minor, rather than a major or medium, influence on their religious development may be no more than a proper judiciousness on their part. Quite a few other things are just more significant in most people's religious development.

A CLASS MASS

It was Advent and the sophomores (15-year-olds) were to meet in their home-room groups for a Mass led by Fr A, the chaplain. I was lucky to catch the first of these. Some 15 boys, the Chaplain, the school Principal who had dropped in, your researcher and Father A in his street clothes, sat in a semi-circle around the altar in a small chapel. Three boys had agreed a few days before to select a reading each and say why they had chosen it. First came the 'light of the world' verses from St Matthew, chosen because 'that's what we're supposed to be'. Then the feeding of the 5,000 because 'we have to feed and help other people'. Finally the golden calf episode from Exodus because 'God is always there for us' – He did forgive the Israelites! Fr A then briefly revisits these readings and comments.

What then followed struck this participant observer as fairly remarkable. The whole group had been asked in their previous Religion class to think about two single things: a present they would particularly like to receive and a present they would particularly like to give at Christmas. Now Fr A kicked off and then each of us (the Principal not flinching and I not daring to) said our pieces in turn. A few boys indicated that they were not quite ready and came in later. Many of the wanted 'gifts' referred to academic work – to be less lazy, to learn not to procrastinate with assignments and so forth. And many of the gifts to be given related to family, for example, to allow for Dad's tiredness when tempted to give him a hard time, or when tempted to give him a hard time back. The atmosphere throughout these 'confessions' was soulful, serious, moral, humble, and relaxed.

Half an hour had passed in this unconventional 'liturgy of the Word' and now the last ten minutes of the single class-period is given over to an abbreviated Eucharistic service: consecration, Lord's Prayer, communion and one minute of silent reflection.

Those boys would not have a similar kind of Mass again that year. They would have some other Eucharistic experiences at school, a year Mass at Thanksgiving, a few whole-school Masses, perhaps a Sunday Mass for the football team before a game, a Mass with their retreat group and so on, but the programme is actually quite a sparing one, and this is a deliberate policy. In a later interview Fr A emphasised the need to do it well, for an occasion or when there was something to celebrate, and not as a routine.

As with RE, the sample of older students would generally identify school liturgies as a minor influence on their religious development and, again, this assessment seems judicious. However impressive they may be – and the engagement of the students in that class Mass had been clear – they are occasional events. It may be of more concern from a Catholic point of view that though 60 per cent of the sample attend their parish churches more or less regularly, and a similar proportion believe Jesus Christ is present in the Eucharist, the sample generally identified the parish as also no more than a minor influence on their development and only a third of them found church services other than boring. Fr A, who anticipated this finding, was at once wholly sympathetic to the student view of the average parish and liturgy, committed to students coming to see themselves as the ones to improve them, and concerned about how realistic this goal was.

RETREATS, FAITH AND SPIRITUAL VALUES

Another, and more heartening, line of exploration opened up from the class Mass. In his interview Fr A remarked that the boys' capacity to share in the personal way I had witnessed did not 'come out of the blue'. They had learnt it in particular, he said, in the group retreats they had already experienced in their 15 months at the school. I would not be at the school long enough to observe a retreat but I learnt that this kind of reflective, quasi-confessional interaction in small groups, sometimes extending to faculty and/or parents, was integral to it. This is captured in the title of the programme for the two top years: the 'Emmaus' Programme.

The retreat programme as a whole at St Simon's is quite unusually extensive and varied, especially in the upper school, and it is constantly being experimented with. In each of the first two years it is a single day together at an out-of-school location, 'getting used to the way of sharing' in preparation for the upper school retreats. The latter – now optional but the great majority of students, including non-Catholics, go – are in groups of six for three days and are based on themes from the Spiritual Exercises. Seniors who have done an Emmaus retreat the previous year can act as leaders of groups along with teachers and/or parents. I was told also of Fireside retreats at camp-sites, father–son retreats, mother–son retreats and of projected brother–brother retreats. At a recent father–son retreat, a boy and his father had engaged together on a variation on the Ignatian death-bed meditation: what would they say to each other if they knew they were going to die that night? When that father really did die soon afterwards the family read from the notes they had kept. At a later mass in the school for the dead man the son preached a homily, using these memories and notes as a basis.

The programme is not just for the students. Many staff act as participant-leaders in the student retreats. A recent development was *Prayer 2000*. A young Jesuit history teacher had just proposed an adaptation of the *Spiritual Exercises* in which they would be stretched out over several months of 'normal life' – and 25 seniors and six faculty had signed up. There is also an annual faculty retreat and the school subsidises staff who want to do a private retreat. Such exercises are seen as close to the core of staff-development at the school – which, as well as more conventional things, also includes – particularly for new staff – informal study-groups led by the Principal to consider the life and spirit of St Ignatius and contemporary developments in the Jesuit view of education.

Granted the occasional character of retreats, one might have expected the questionnaire sample to rate them as also a minor influence on their religious development. In fact, they emerged as a major influence (Flynn, 1993: medium influence), a distinction shared only with 'parental lives and example'. Eighty to 90 per cent of the sample thought it at least probable that their last retreat was not boring, taught them respect for the views of others, gave them a sense of self-worth, had brought them close to God at times, and had had a lasting influence on them. Half or more were certain of each of these things. They were well ahead of the 'medium' influences of peer-group, Catholic schooling, and teachers (Flynn: minor, if not negative, influence).

In round figures, 90 per cent of the sample believed in God, 80 per cent that God is a loving Father, 70 per cent that 'God always forgives me', 55 per cent that Jesus is truly God (but just 10 per cent that he is not) and 70 per cent that 'Jesus is very close to me'. Fifty per cent believe that it is important to pray each day and 75 per cent do actually pray more or less regularly. On a more or less regular basis, 60 per cent attend Mass outside school, 55 per cent go to confession and 50 per cent read scripture. Fifty-five per cent acknowledged the life-goal of finding 'God in my life and growing in faith in Him' and only 6 per cent rejected it. We may surmise that these are among the beliefs and practices in which the retreat programme tended seriously to confirm them. There is a view in the faculty that there is also some carry-over from the retreat programme to other aspects of the school and the lives of the students. Thus the Principal opined – when asked how Ignatian was the school – that, among other things:

> these kids become reflective, academically and otherwise, beyond the usual; they tended not to take rash decisions, to be careful thinkers, thoughtful thinkers.

THE COMMUNITY SERVICE LEARNING PROGRAMME

George runs the Community Service Programme for sophomore students at the school. Some such programme has run for at least 25 years, but it has evolved. The latest change has been to increase the requirement from 30 to 50 hours so as further to discourage kids from getting it over in a 'one-shot' 4/5 day burst – the preferred rhythm is once or twice a week for two to three hours at a time. Students usually find their own placement and get parental authorisation but their choices have to be approved by George. The main criterion is that it should involve them in the direct and more or less continuous service of others. Projects range through working at homeless shelters, working in hospitals and tutoring young kids free of charge. They put in the hours in their own time, not school-time, but while engaged on these projects they also attend a weekly session of debriefing and discussion with George or one of the other teachers involved. Usually, they keep a journal, and they prepare a presentation of their project for their group. They tell and they listen – and they readily move on to causes and structures.

> A kid may be excited to realise that the homeless are not bums, but as broad a range as you'll get; some had very good jobs; this can happen to anyone.

What adds to the challenge is that there are always some kids who are puzzled and resentful at this 'forced volunteering'. They have to be dragged 'kicking and screaming' into it, but, George adds, if the processes are good it turns around for them and they generally agree by the end that it was worthwhile. George and other interviewees were pretty sure the programme had long-term effects on most of the participants, at the least, that it is one of those things in the school – alongside, for example, such curricular initiatives as the close study of immigration policy in American history – that inclines alumni 'to vote not just for themselves but for other people'.[5]

Questionnaire returns in this area were inconclusive. Eighty per cent try to be friendly and helpful to the rejected and lonely and two-thirds are positively concerned about the homeless and disadvantaged. On the other hand, in regard to both their expectations of the school and their personal life-goals, socio-political altruism, though acknowledged, scored markedly lower for the sample as a whole than either personal fulfillment or career success. Ignatian people, mindful of their meditation on original sin, may find themselves more encouraged by the acknowledgment than disappointed at the lower priority!

THE SCHOOL AS COMMUNITY

The school seemed a happy and busy place as I moved about in it and it was noticeable how many interviewees spontaneously expressed their regard for their colleagues and, very particularly, their students. But it was the student questionnaires, which systematically canvassed views on the school ethos, that yielded the more sustained and dramatic evidence of strong community. In a section headed 'School Life and Climate', the sample used a five-point scale to respond to a series of 36 statements expressing feelings and views regarding their school, its ethos, and its teachers. Their overall response was quite formidably positive (significantly more so than Flynn's already strongly positive findings). It may be summarised as follows (using round figures):

- *Perception of their own feelings:* Ninety per cent had been happy at school, 70 per cent felt accepted by other students and 75 per cent felt they were treated with respect. Their school was not a place where they felt lonely (90 per cent), or depressed (80 per cent), or worried (70 per cent). Adequate counselling help was available (85 per cent).

- *Community-spirit:* The Principal encouraged community and a sense of belonging (85 per cent), most teachers knew their final-year students as individuals and showed a good deal of school spirit (70 per cent), most students are friendly (75 per cent), everyone welcomes you (70 per cent), there was a good spirit of community in their own senior year (85 per cent), and there is a happy atmosphere in the school (80 per cent).

- *Evaluation of the school:* Their school has a good name in the local community (95 per cent), they feel proud to be at it (85 per cent), students generally think a lot of it (80 per cent). Teachers are well qualified and good, and take time to help students in difficulty with their school work (90 per cent), most teachers go out of their way to help (75 per cent) and carry out their work with energy and pleasure (65 per cent), relations between staff and parents are very friendly (70 per cent), and they can approach the Principal for advice and help (60 per cent, with just 15 per cent disagreeing).

- *Discipline:* Students know the standard of conduct expected (90 per cent), discipline presents no real problem (60 per cent, just 15 per cent voting definitely the other way) and – rather significantly – their school rules encourage self-discipline and responsibility (85 per cent).

- *Catholicity of the school:* The Principal values the religious nature of the school and the Catholic teachers set an example of what it means to be a practising Catholic (70 per cent). (There was less confidence that student colleagues understood and accepted the religious goals of the school.) They would attend a Catholic school if they 'had to do it all over again' (70 per cent) and would cheerfully visit this fate on their future children (80 per cent).

For all these items, the proportions of uncomplimentary, as opposed to non-commital, responses was less than 20 per cent in virtually all cases and less that 10 per cent in many cases.

In their responses to suggested life goals, the sample gave pride of place to Fulfilment and Relationship Goals over both Success Goals and Religious-Spiritual Goals. Personal happiness, self-acceptance, a happy marriage and family life, and lifelong friendships, in that order, were judged most, or very, important goals by larger numbers than *any* of the suggested goals in the other categories. We may surmise that this emphasis owes something to their experience of the St Simon's ethos.

NOTES

1. The study is one of a series of studies of 'good' Catholic schools in seven countries that is currently being undertaken by the author and a colleague.
2. Now amended to *men and women with and for others* this has become a useful 'slogan' description of the desired product that is now omnipresent in Jesuit literature and schools.
3. Coincidentally, I offered a philosophical account and justification of such an educational goal in Walsh (1993), chs 8ff., see below.
4. A series of 13 questionnaire items offered a quite subtle test of the respondents' knowledge and 'feel' in relation to Catholic terms and teachings, on which the sample of 47 achieved a creditable average of 65 per cent. Their average scores for questions relating to the role of conscience and to attitudes to the world exceeded 80 per cent.
5. O'Keefe and McCafferty (1995) found a positive medium-term (three to six years) influence of this kind of programme in Jesuit High Schools.

REFERENCES

Flynn, M. (1993) *The Culture of Catholic Schools: A Study of Catholic Schools 1972–1993*. St Pauls, Homebush, New South Wales.

Hamilton, D. (1989) *Towards a Theory of Schooling*: London: Falmer.

Hamilton, D. (1990) *Learning about Education: An Unfinished Curriculum.* Milton Keynes, Open University Press.

International Commission on Jesuit Education (1987), 'Go Forth to Teach, The Characteristics of Jesuit Education', republished in Meirose (ed.) (1994).

Meirose, C. (ed.) (1994) *Foundations.* Washington, DC, The Jesuit Secondary Education Assoc.

O'Keefe, J. and McCafferty, P. (1995) 'Beyond Noblesse Oblige: Community Service Learning in High School', paper presented at the Annual Meeting of the American Educational Research Association.

Walsh. P. (1993) *Education and Meaning: Philosophy in Practice.* London, Cassell.

11

GLOBAL PERSPECTIVES AND EDUCATION IN VALUES

Roy Gardner

Few people would perhaps be opposed to the need to reduce the indebtedness of countries in the South and of the urgency of removing the mountainous burden of the repayments required to service the debts. The *Guardian* (12 May 1998) asserted that 21 million children in Africa, Asia and Latin America will die because of the debts. Millions more will grow up unable to read or write because government budgets for health and education are dwarfed by debt repayments to the West. Such a situation is appalling and it is no wonder that there has been a movement among the wealthier nations to mark the millennium by the cancellation of debt. However, even if there were agreement on a mechanism for such a gesture towards the relief of over-burdened economies to provide an opportunity for poorer countries to refocus their development strategies, many might argue that it would raise ethical dilemmas which cannot be settled easily by the stroke of a pen. The wealthier nations could afford to cancel debt but the arguments against the cancellation would be based on the proposition that it would represent a paternalistic action which is ill-suited to the independence and maturity of the debtor countries. The debts were incurred either through trade agreements or through aid loans. Each of these agreements was reached through negotiation and settlement between sovereign countries who understood fully the obligations which the debts carried. To cancel the debts might therefore be interpreted as treating the debtors in an indulgent and patronising way.

The question of Third World indebtedness raises many issues which are very relevant to the teaching of global issues. The origin of the debts, the purposes for which they were incurred, the mechanisms of repayment and the role of the debts in national development are all important facets of the unequal, unfair world which global learning seeks to illuminate. None of the elements listed above are simple and many involve complexities which require careful analysis. Taken together the elements represent highly significant factors in the continued low level of development of many of the countries of the South. Yet what should be the approach to be adopted in the schools when the question of debt is raised prominently in the media and in international fora of how to work towards a more equitable world for 2000 and beyond?

The teaching about debt can and should be dealt with at different levels for differing groups of learners, be they in school or out of it. At one level, the debt could be compared to personal debt between members of a family or to others, and pupils could be asked to examine the ethics of having a debt and expecting it to be cancelled without paying it back. Family commitment to mortgages, car repayments, hire purchase and so forth might provide a useful parallel on the personal level to examine how families might feel burdened or indeed in reality be burdened by debt which restricts their freedom of action and leaves them with little disposable income. At another level, the level of repayments on debt could be re-examined in the light of the interest rates that have been charged and the final amount that would have to be paid to clear the debt in relation to the original level of the debt. At what point might the individual, the family or a country decide that enough has been repaid of the principal and interest to wipe out the debt, i.e. at what point do the repayments become 'unfair'? For the creditor, presumably never, unless, through an act of magnanimity, the creditor unilaterally decides to cancel. At yet a further level, analysis of the impact of debt repayments on national disposable income might show the extent of the burden and a need for an overwhelming restructuring to ensure that development does go ahead and the country does not regress with declining standards of living.

This limited foray into the world of multilateral and bilateral aid with or without tied trade agreements has been intended to illustrate one of the most enduring and pervasive difficulties which face the teaching of world issues. Complex questions have been raised at many stages over the last 25 years and pupils in schools have been required to absorb, analyse and conclude upon them. The degree to which those students have been able to carry out the process required has, of course, varied with the age at which they have been asked to engage with situations which have in many cases been highly emotional. The ability to undertake any world-wide analysis has been highly circumscribed by the detail of the data available, the degree to which any objectivity could be brought to the study and, equally importantly, the time available in school for the work to be undertaken.

GLOBAL PERSPECTIVES IN THE NATIONAL CURRICULUM

Much of what has been described so far represents early efforts to teach about the contrasts between countries, the inequalities and the iniquities which exist in the modern-day world. Efforts they were and they did not easily coalesce into a major focus in the provision made for pupils in the compulsory phase of education. What has been needed, and still is, is a conception of the place of teaching about global issues in the curriculum for young people aged 5 to 16 and beyond.

The questions of debt, of unequal development, of wealth and poverty existing side by side with protestations of the equality of mankind raise larger ones still of what are the aims of education as a whole within compulsory education. With Walsh (1993, p. 92) we might query why it is thought right and important to have (consciously) and to hand on (deliberately) a view of life as a whole. Walsh asks us to reflect on the satirical scene at the end of *Monty Python: The Meaning of Life*. After the caption 'The End' the camera returns to John Cleese who says, 'That is the end of the film. Here is the meaning of life. Nothing very special really! Be kind, avoid eating too much fat, read a good book now and then, get in some walking – oh, and live in peace and harmony with people of all nations, races and creeds!' Walsh in assessing this question reflects on 'curriculum, in particular, the "core curriculum"'. He argues that 'as "commmon core" it is charged with articulating and enabling our common social life and citizenship, indeed our common humanity'. Halstead (1996) has also asked us to consider what are the distinctively human qualities essential to being more fully a person (p. 112).

Within a national curriculum there is need for a definition or at least an explanation of the purpose of education which goes beyond the expression of structures and the contents of subjects. There is place for an expression of the type of person who should emerge from the educational process not only in knowledge, understandings and skills but also in terms of attitudes or values. White (1995) has argued that religious educators have claimed they help children to locate themselves in the universe as a whole. White asks, 'Cannot the secular cosmic framework provide for the wider conception of human well-being and their place in the universe which children need?'

With the pace of change in the modern world and its expected exponential growth there is serious concern that individuals will become disoriented in their approach to life and living. Gellner (1992) argues:

> In a stable traditional world, men had identities, linked to their social roles, and confirmed by their overall vision of nature and society. Instability and change both in knowledge and society have deprived such self-images of their erstwhile feel of reliability. Identities are perhaps more ironic and conditional than once they were, or at any rate, when confident, unjustifiably so. (p. 182)

Global perspectives, world issues, development education and a host of other names each point to the need for a broad area of study in the national curriculum. This area is thought to be presented best by a theme which runs across subjects. Concern has been expressed about the value of cross-curricular themes and note might be taken of the analysis by Ahier (1995).

> Just as there are vital disagreements within the academic subjects which inform these themes, these public concerns are not defined in a consensual way either. There are very definite divisions between the groups who construct these debates. For example, behind what might be described as the environmental lobby lie a number of serious disagreements on theory, philosophy, tactics, strategy and political perspective ... Unfortunately the documents ... identify no major differences of informed opinion about economic or environmental matters, no 'schools of thought', no theoretical or ideological conflicts. The documents' 'coyness' about what one might call organised oppositions means they can suggest no ways in which teachers within a democratic society should deal with such disagreements and differences. (pp. 140–1)

Beck (1998, p. 98) goes on to note that Ahier's argument is all the more disturbing since the raison d'être of cross-curricular themes such as Environmental Education and Education for Citizenship is their direct relevance to everday life – in its public as well as its private dimensions. Ahier concludes:

> If ... cross-curricular themes are curricular constructions which are built on or reflect major public concerns, then it is imporant to determine the extent to which the guidance offered reflects the range of positions expressed within those concerns. (p. 147)

APPROACHES TO TEACHING GLOBAL PERSPECTIVES

Development education has long wrestled with the problems and difficulties of representing adequately the basic question of world development in the classroom. The earliest attempts at development education were by those who had worked in countries in the South for a number of years, probably as volunteers, and who on return to teaching in the UK wanted to share their knowledge and experience with their charges. These attempts brought vivid images of faraway places, although none of them could have been charged with claims of aid pornography (Harrison, 1998). These initiatives soon led to more detailed analyses of the world stage which could provide image, documentation and detail. Global analyses of the distribution of population, agricultural production, industrial production, levels of consumption, coupled with statements of gross national income per capita, led rapidly to the recognition of inequality. It led also to the emergence of the concept of the North and the South and the associations of affluence and poverty which those names confirmed.

Soon also came the realisation that such analyses, which provided a broad understanding of global distribution and trends, did little to help the individual learner understand their significance in the daily lives of those living in poverty in the South. There emerged an approach to undertake a detailed study of a small part of a country to appreciate not only the minutiae of life but also its precariousness. Those studies were valuable illustrations but illustrative of who and what? On what basis were the studies selected? How representative were they of the country from which they were selected, of a region, or continent or the developing world? At best these small-scale studies were appropriate for the areas studied but not elsewhere: and time did not allow for the exercise to be repeated in a range of situations and countries to provide an acceptable coverage of the reality of life in the South. Moreover, such studies could have provided a biased view focusing on the difficulties of life perhaps in a rural area, not the better situation in the towns. Perhaps also the studies were not always able to capture the joys of life in many countries but tended to concentrate on the hardships, the tragedies and the relentlessness of the oppression the natural environment foisted upon the individual and the community.

TOWARDS A DEFINITION OF GLOBAL PERSPECTIVES IN EDUCATION

Numerous attempts have been made to define global perspectives and development education and a review of these definitions may be instructive at this stage.

In 1975 the United Nations issued a statement about the purpose of development education which included a significant reference to human rights.

> Development education is concerned with issues of human rights, dignity, self-reliance, and social justice in both developed and developing countries. It is concerned with the causes of underdevelopment and the promotion of an understanding of what is involved in development, of how different countries go about undertaking development, and of the reasons for and ways of achieving a new international economic and social order. (cited in Hicks and Townley, 1982)

The introduction of human rights into the equation provided the opportunity for a substantive review of approaches and activities. For most people, perhaps, human rights has meant fundamental freedoms against arbitrary imprisonment, torture and execution and freedoms of speech, assembly and participation. Article 26-2 of the Universal Declaration of Human Rights went further and targeted education as a vital component in the provision of human rights:

> Education should be directed to the full development of the human personality and to the strengthening of respect for human rights and fundamental freedoms. It should promote understanding, tolerance and friendship among all nations, races and religious groups and shall further the articles of the United Nations for the maintenance of peace.

This view of the role of education in human rights and a world view of development and growth mirrored much of what had been happening in British schools. The need to engage learners with situations which took them away from their own immediate concerns had been a focus of much of the developmental work that had already been taking place. That work had stressed the opportunities which existed to encourage empathy for people in other parts of the world and especially those who were less fortunate in terms of the availability of basic resources to satisfy their everyday needs. What the introduction of human rights did was to broaden the agenda leading to the concept of a global citizenry to which each individual belongs and has a duty to contribute. As globalisation has gripped the lives of us all and the imagination of educationalists, there has been a significant increase in the statements made to guide learning. Thus the Development Education Association sees development education as encompassing the following principles:

- enabling young people to understand the links between their own lives and those of people throughout the world;
- increasing understanding of the economic, social, political and environmental factors which shape our lives;
- developing skills, attitudes and values which enable people to work together to bring about change and take control of their lives;
- working towards achieving a more just and sustainable world in which power and resources are more equitably shared.

This has been strengthened further by UNESCO (1997) with its stress on the close relationship between human rights and development education and by Barber (1998).

> Whatever else the school system in a country like ours achieves, the bottom line should be that it needs to strive to create a generation which is not only well-educated in the core academic sense, but also has a highly developed sense of ethics and of global as well as national citizenship.

This view reflects also that of the Commission on Global Governance (1995) which expressed the urgent need for a global ethic and of Larcher (1991) who pointed to the importance of intercultural learning in developing a greater openness towards other countries as a means of overcoming culture bias and ethnocentrism (p. 62).

These statements have provided a framework upon which to build a new co-ordinated programme of global perspectives and much effort has been expended in attempts to elaborate appropriate schemes, along with differing arguments used to justify teaching about development and human rights. Osler and Starkey (1998) have suggested that the teaching of human rights can be used as an antidote to postmodernism. They draw attention to Ferry's (Ferry and Renault, 1988) view that postmodernism is an individualistic philosophy which embraces 'the spontaneous, the anarchic, the irrational, the emotional and the archaic' (p. 5). Postmodernism does not countenance normative statements of values and this creates considerable, if not insurmountable differences, in teaching about world issues in schools and elsewhere. Without an agreed set of goals and objectives for economic and social development the prospect of teaching towards greater equality in the world becomes dire. The acceptance of a basic set of values globally would be impossible under postmodernism, as would the rejection of practices such as torture, violence and female circumcision. These could be claimed to be acceptable because they were traditional parts of the fabric of life. Development education on the other hand seeks to articulate an overarching moral code based on rationality and compassion for all fellow human beings.

Other claims for the place of global education in schools are based on the guidelines issued by government agencies. The Education Reform Act (1988) made no mention of global perspectives but OFSTED issued the following in 1994.

Children should have:

- knowledge of literature and roots of their own cultural traditions and practices and the key features of other major cultural groups in their society;
- understanding of the diversity of religious, social, aesthetic, ethnic and political traditions, nationally and internationally.

This provided a stimulus to the formulation of ideas and at least one author was sufficiently enthusiastic to suggest that the whole curriculum should consist of:

3 R's: Reading, Writing and the Rest of the Word (Brownlie, 1998)

One starting point for any new proposal for curriculum content should always be a review of current knowledge and understanding of the learners. Speed, Kent and Byron on behalf of DEA MORI (1998) conducted a survey of 11–16-year-olds and the findings provide valuable guidelines for curriculum planners:

Summary of findings

- Most pupils feel they know something about global and development issues. The causes of war are the topic young people are most inclined to say they understand to some degree (72%), while around two in three feel they have some insight into the reasons behind environmental destruction, famine and over-population. In general, older pupils feel more knowledgeable than younger ones.

- The causes of war, along with the reasons for human rights abuses, also emerge as issues that young people are particularly inclined to say they want to learn about. In total, just under half say they would like to know more about each of these topics.

- Seven in ten pupils agree that people in this age group should learn more about global issues; few actively disagree (6%).

- Television (82%) is cited as the primary source of information about developmental issues, especially among older pupils. Other sources referred to by at least half are: school (74%), newspapers (64%), and parents (57%). Boys are more likely than girls to mention using the Internet in this context.

- The vast majority of pupils believe it is important to learn about global issues at school (81%), and that young people need to understand global matters in order to make choices about how to lead their lives (81%).

- Change in working practices is the factor – from a list of five – that young people are least likely to think will seriously affect them in their daily lives (74%). Only one in eight thinks that this will have a limited impact. At least half think it likely that each of the other four items will have an impact: environmental disasters (65%), war (62%), the increasing gap between rich and poor countries (61%), and natural disasters (58%).

This survey shows that pupils do have some knowledge about a limited range of issues but would wish to know more about them and others. School does provide a vital source of knowledge and the education system does have the opportunity to provide more information and promote understanding to help young people make appropriate choices about their lives. Media studies courses also provide a useful vehicle for developmental issues. Television was acknowledged by the respondents as their prime source of learning, bearing in mind the time already spent viewing programmes.

Much has been said in the past as to whether global issues should be a subject in the curriculum in schools or represented by themes across the curriculum but there appears to be general agreement today that the area of study would best be presented by an infusion in subjects. The careful selection of teaching materials would ensure that pupils were exposed to development issues and that equal attention was paid to processes. A skills-based approach to development has been called for and OXFAM (1998) has provided a detailed analysis for global citizenship which may be used as a basis for curriculum development incorporating knowledge and understanding, skills, and values and attitudes. This framework is elaborated to provide foci for sub-categories across the key stages and a sample is given in Table 11.1.

TABLE 11.1
Curriculum for Global Citizenship Knowledge and Understanding

	Pre-KSI	KS1 5–7	KS2 7–11	KS3 11–14	KS4 14–16	16–19
Knowledge and understanding	What's fair or unfair	Awareness of rich or poor	Fairness between groups	Inequalities within and between societies	Causes of poverty	Understanding of global debates
Social justice and equality	What's right or wrong		Causes and effects of inequality	Basic rights and responsibilities	Different views on the eradication of poverty. Role as a global citizen	
Diversity	Awareness of others in relation to self. Understanding similarities and differences between people	Greater awareness of similarities and differences between people	Contribution of different cultures, values and beliefs in our lives. Nature of prejudice and ways to combat it	Understanding of issues of diversity	Deeper understanding of different cultures and societies	

DfEE and QCA have provided a report from the Panel for Education and Sustainable Development in the Schools Sector (1998) which adopts seven key concepts as a framework for curriculum design. These are:

- interdependence – of society, economy and the natural environment from local to global;
- citizenship and stewardship – rights and responsibilities, participation, and co-operation;
- needs and rights of future generations;
- diversity – culture, social, economic and biological;
- quality of life, equity and justice;
- sustainable change – development and the carrying capacity;
- uncertainty and precaution in action.

Each key concept is further developed in a matrix with Values and Dispositions; Skills and Aptitudes; Knowledge and Understanding. This formulation together with that offered by OXFAM provides a rich source for planning whether it be at the school, local or national level.

CONCLUSION

Any curriculum innovation needs not only a clear focus but also statements of expected outcomes. Both OXFAM and the Panel for Education for Sustainable Development have provided valuable statements. However there needs to be a set of measures which can be used to assess the effectiveness of global education. McCollum (1998) has outlined some of the challenges facing development education and has expressedly focused on its impact on the learners. Bottani and Walberg (1992) have stressed the need for information and benchmarks that would permit comparison for and indicators of how well global education is functioning. Such indicators would be a valuable tool for the improvement of the quality of both global learning and the whole educational experiences of the learner. Perhaps the next step in the debate would be to define in precise and measurable terms the sorts of gains that learners would be expected to exhibit at specified times throughout their learning period in schools.

To recap, the questions so far raised about the nature and teaching of global education are:

- to what extent should development/global education contribute to an overarching view of the purposes of education within any national education system? and:
- is it possible to teach effectively development/global education within an education system devoid of common goals?
- how far should development/global education seek to engage pupils with the differing, indeed opposing, views involved in the realpolitik of global development?
- if so, in what ways might teachers be assisted in the teaching of the controversial issues surrounding this key focus for the development of young people within the post-modernist, poorly signposted ethical and moral areas of social and personal life choices?

Educators do need guidance in seeking to develop their students and it may be useful to attempt to define the characteristics of the desirable person who has been provided with international dimensions in the curriculum. Such a paradigmatic graduand of the school system might:

- Be aware of the approximate location of countries and continents on the globe and different ways of representing them on a map.

- Be aware that there are very many groups of people who have languages, customs, values and beliefs and religions different from the majority who live in the UK.
- Whilst understanding and appreciating his/her own culture, its origins and changing patterns, would also respect and attempt to understand other cultures and the implications of these cultures on daily life styles.
- Be aware of the diversity of characteristics within other countries and be willing to adopt a broad approach to the study of individual countries.
- Be aware of the contribution of other peoples and civilisations to development through literature, inventions and innovations in the sciences and especially medicine.
- Be aware of different interpretations of 'development', processes of development and the factors which may promote or inhibit development.
- Be aware of the importance of the world's environment and resources and the need to manage these sustainably.
- Be aware of the interdependence of economies and countries and to appreciate the impact of industrial and trade policies.
- Be aware of the inequalities in the distribution and consumption of goods and services around the world, of alternative explanations of those inequalities and the need for action to reduce them.
- Be aware of the work of international organisations, aid agencies, non-governmental agencies and of the politics of aid.
- Be aware of cultural bias and the perpetuation of stereotypes in the media. (Gardner, 1990)

No doubt this description will attract comment because of its focus on awareness. However it may be argued that awareness is all one could reasonably expect of learners during the compulsory phase of education. This would not satisfy many writers (see Osler, 1994, p. 2). Apart from the practical difficulties of arranging for on-going forms of action, Hopkin (1990) would question the value of young learners participating in activities the purpose of which they may not fully understand and to which they might contribute solely as part of a school routine. Schools might establish the need for action to be taken but expect this to be coupled with understanding and commitment when the learners have economic and political capability.

Finally perhaps educators might find it useful to use Kenneth

Boulding's (see Ellyard file://A:\ellyard,htm) metaphor of the need of the Earth to change from a 'cowboy economy' to a 'spaceship economy' to ensure survival. Boulding thought the nineteenth century was characterised by dependence, the twentieth one by independence but the twenty-first should be one characterised by interdependence on a networked planet: 'Interdependence is a keyword to describe our evolving just-in-time, environmentally sensitive society: interdependence between men and women, between tribes and nations, between enterprises, between employer and employee in our work places, and between humanity and nature.'

Perhaps students could be encouraged to adopt the spaceship culture and explore in their learning about planet Earth how we may benefit from our interdependence. Perhaps now as globalisation gathers pace and young people become more familiar with the internet, a realisation of the need for cooperation and of the reality of interdependence may usher in the era of global thinking that so many have sought to instil through their teaching in the past.

REFERENCES

Ahier, J. (1995) 'Hidden Controversies in Two Cross-Curricular Themes', in J. Ahier and A. Ross (eds), *The Social Subjects within the Curriculum: Children's Social Learning within the National Curriculum*. London, Falmer.

Barber, M. (1998) Address to Secondary Headteachers Association Conference.

Beck, J (1998) *Morality and Citizenship in Education*. London, Cassell.

Bottani, N. and Walberg, H. (1992), 'What are International Education Indicators for?', in *OECD International Education Indicators: A Framework for Analysis*. Paris, OECD.

Brownlie, A. (1998) *Guardian*, 1 January.

Commission on Global Governance (1995) *Our Global Neighbourhood*. Oxford, Oxford University Press.

DEA (1999–2002) 'The Challenge of the Global Society: A Strategy for Development Education into the Millennium', London, Development Education Association.

Ferry, L. and Renault, A. (1988) *La Pensée 68*. Paris, Gallimard.

Gardner, R (ed.) (1990) *An International Dimension in the Curriculum: An Imperative for Britain for 1992 and Beyond*. London, London Institute of Education.

Gellner, E. (1992) *Reason and Culture: The Historic Role of Rationality and Rationalism*. Oxford, Blackwell.

Halstead, J.M. and Taylor, M.J. (eds) (1996) *Values in Education and Education in Values*. London, Falmer.

Harrison, B. (1998) 'Is this Aid Pornography?', *Guardian*, 29 May.

Hicks, D. and Townley, C. (1982) *Teaching World Studies: An Introduction to Global Pedagogy in the Curriculum*. Harlow, Longman.

Hopkin, A. (1990) 'An International Dimension and Public Examination', in R. Gardner (ed.), *An International Dimension in the National Curriculum: An Imperative for Britain for 1992 and Beyond*. London, London Institute of Education.

Larcher, D. (1991) *Fremde in der Nähe*. Klagenfürst, Drava.

McCollum, A. (1998) 'Some Evaluation Challenges Facing Development Education', DEA July, vol. 5, 1 October.

Osler, A. (ed.) (1994) *Development Education: Global Perspectives in the Curriculum*. London, Cassell.

Osler, A. and Starkey, H. (1998) Development, Human Rights and the Teaching of Values. DEA July, vol. 4, 2 February.

OXFAM (1998) 'A Curriculum for Global Citizenship: A Guide for Teachers and Education Workers', Oxford, OXFAM.

Panel for Education and Sustainable Development (1998) 'Education for Sustainable Development in the Schools Sector: A Report to DFEE/QCA', London, DEA.

Speed, M., Kent, A. and Byron, A. (1998), 'Children's Knowledge of Global Issues: A Research Study among 11–16 Year Olds', London, DEA/MORI.

UNESCO (1997) *European Implementation Strategy on the UN Declaration of Human Rights Education*. Paris, UNESCO.

Walsh, P. (1993) *Education and Meaning: Philosophy in Practice*. London, Cassell.

White, J (1995) *Institute of Education Society Newsletter*, 10(1), London Institute of Education, University of London.

Part V:

A Perspective for the Future

12

HOW CAN RESEARCH INTO EDUCATION IN VALUES HELP SCHOOL PRACTICE?

Monica Taylor

Values in education and public life have recently gained a higher profile and are currently prominent in social and educational debate. Educational policies require schools to give a lead spiritually, morally, socially and culturally in the curriculum and school life, as if schools alone could compensate for the ills of society. There are other influences on the values of the young, which may be congruent, or in tension with those of the school. Young people's values, attitudes, personal qualities and behaviour have probably been of concern in every age, yet a science of school-based values education is only just emerging. In the light of current social concerns, how can research in values education help school practice? To set the scene, I outline the social and educational context for values education and identify some conceptual and practical issues. Several current and ongoing research initiatives on values education are described and a further research agenda for values education is identified. In so doing, I hope to indicate how research and practice are, or should be, integrally connected in order to improve values education in schools.

THE PROFILE OF VALUES EDUCATION

Individual and institutional values concerns – especially moral or ethical concerns – seem to be gaining a higher profile in societies and in the acknowledged challenges to education as we move forward in the new millennium. Why should values be a current educational focus? England is by no means alone in this resurgence of interest. Indeed, some other countries of Western Europe have accorded values education a more continuous curriculum profile and greater resource priority. In an overview of a research survey of values education in 26 European countries, spanning East and West, in 1993, I concluded that there were several common underlying themes which form the social background to contemporary educational efforts in values education (Taylor, 1994a). It is worth summarising these themes here to consider their resonance in an English context.

- *Social crisis* has stemmed from economic insecurity and a hectic pace of social change. In the social values turmoil many are marginalised or disenfranchised, and there is widespread concern about violence, crime, delinquency and the effect of drugs.

- *Pluralism* has burgeoned with increasing social, ethnic and cultural diversity. Whilst for some this seems to be at the root of concerns about relativism, the challenges and enrichment of pluralism are nowhere more evident or demanding than in schools, which can be the meeting point for diversity or reflect the artificiality of segregation. Racism and cultural imperialism remain implicit and explicit in the cultural landscape and as issues in everyday life.

- *Religious influence* and the extent to which religion should have a place in the structure of education systems and curricula is controversial, as we well know from considerations of the role of collective worship. Despite a creeping secularism, there is also a reawakening of interest in the spiritual life, as well as rearguard action from religious groups with traditional values in the face of religious pluralism.

- *Democracy and the promotion of citizenship* have become a rallying point as disenchantment with some Western democratic systems and with political and industrial corruption have led to a common call for the encouragement of active participatory citizenship.

- *Nationalism and national identity* as expressed in contrasting country responses, directly related to recent experiences of domination, or the need to forge a nation state from diverse peoples, show that there are powerful forces supporting the development of national identity, patriotism and the revival or transmission of cultural traditions. At the same time, there is also debate about the development of a European identity as many countries become more connected in the European Union.

These social and cultural changes give rise to concerns and challenges to be reinterpreted in a country's structural response to values education in the light of the historical and ideological background to its education system (for a descriptive overview of England, see Taylor, 1994b).

In the social context of England in Britain, a certain moral panic has not surprisingly been engendered by several recent destructive, anti-social, immoral, terrifying and horrifying acts perpetrated by adults or young people in or around schools themselves: the machete attack at Dunblane, the murder of Philip Lawrence. In particular, the nation's conscience was stirred by the abduction and killing of a toddler, James Bulger, by two boys of primary school age. More generally, media reports of child abuse, rape, murder become almost commonplace, alongside those of political, financial and commercial corruption. Our own observations of everyday life, as we move about the capital, our communities, and in our family lives and workplaces provide us with many disquieting ethical concerns (Taylor, 1997a) and, if we have an enduring interest in values, we have readily to mind examples from many narratives and conversations. Indeed, if we listen, we find that values issues form the stuff of daily dialogue and on-going lifelong learning.

Educationally, whilst schools have traditionally aimed at the personal, social and academic development of the individual, a new values era seemed to dawn with the 1988 Reform Act which explicitly required schools to provide a broad and balanced curriculum, paying attention to 'spiritual, moral and cultural ... development of pupils at the school and of society' in order to prepare young people for 'the opportunities, responsibilities and experiences of adult life' (GB. Statutes, 1988, Section 1 (2)). This catalyst was followed by various forms of non-statutory guidance. First, that on *The Whole Curriculum*, which seemed to give the green light to personal autonomy, within certain bounds, 'The educational system ... has a duty to educate [the] individuals to think and act for themselves, with an acceptable set of personal qualities and values which also meet the wider social demands of adult life' (NCC, 1990a, p. 7). Secondly, the cross-curricular themes, especially that of citizenship, made clear reference to values. *Education for Citizenship*, stated 'pupils should be helped to develop a personal moral code and to explore values and beliefs. Shared values, such as concern for others, industry and effort, self-respect and self-discipline, as well as moral qualities, such as honesty and truthfulness, should be promoted...' (NCC, 1990b, p. 4). However, since the cross-curricular themes are non-statutory, schools have largely failed to give them much priority in an already overloaded curriculum, and they experience constraints on delivery, such as timetabling, resourcing and staff expertise (Saunders, Hewitt and MacDonald, 1995).

Later, in 1993, the NCC issued a discussion document on *Spiritual and Moral Development,* which, in particular, encouraged schools to develop a whole-school approach, and a values statement 'which sets out the values the school intends to promote and which it intends to demonstrate through aspects of its life' (NCC, 1993, p. 7). This document was also forthright about the list of moral values schools should include: 'telling the truth; keeping promises; respecting the rights and property of others; acting considerately towards others; helping those less fortunate and weaker than ourselves; taking personal responsibility for one's actions; self-discipline.' Conversely and importantly, it also recommended that school values should reject: 'bullying; cheating; deceit; cruelty; irresponsibility; dishonesty' (NCC, 1993, p. 4). By the end of formal schooling, morally educated school leavers should, among other qualities, be able to 'articulate their own attitudes and values ... develop for themselves a set of socially acceptable values and principles, and set guidelines to cover their own behaviour' (p. 5). This phase of curricular guidance may be characterised as one of policy proclamation and exhortation to schools. Lacking statutory force and any resource support, such values pronouncements were of low priority for schools attempting to implement the subjects of the national curriculum, whose values dimensions went largely unperceived.

Arguably the single most propelling influence on schools' reconsideration of their values endeavours has been the statutory requirement that OFSTED inspections report on the spiritual, moral, social and cultural (SMSC) *development* of their pupils (GB Statutes, 1992). That SMSC development initially ranked alongside three other key areas of inspection (quality of education, educational standards and management of educational resources) might have suggested that in principle value – though whether or not it was *equal* value was then unclear – was being placed on these educational aims. Unsurprisingly, however, SMSC development presented challenges of definition, guidance and evaluation for inspectors (OFSTED, 1994a). This led to a refocus on 'opportunities' offered by the school and 'how the pupils respond to that provision' including 'whether pupils are developing their own values' (OFSTED, 1994b). Indeed, in the revised *Framework for the Inspection of Schools* (OFSTED, 1995a) pupils' spiritual, moral, social and cultural development has become subsumed under the heading of quality of education. Despite the guidance issued to inspectors in the *Handbook,* and the fact that inspectors are obliged to consult with parents on whether they are 'happy with the values and attitudes which the school teaches' and to take account of pupils' views, questions have been raised about the shared understanding of criteria and evidence by inspectors, and of the possible simplistic assumption that certain aspects of provision, adult role models and collective worship will necessarily have a positive causal effect on pupil outcomes in terms of values, attitudes and personal qualities. Nevertheless, in spite of this broad brush approach, OFSTED reports, in their own way, provided some of the first 'research' information about the extent and nature of values education. For example, an HMCI report (OFSTED, 1997) states that whereas provision for moral and social development is good, it is much weaker for spiritual development and, in terms of cultural development, 'too little is done, outside of religious education and assembly, to prepare pupils for life in a multicultural society' (p. 17). Key concerns relate to planning, making values explicit in curricular provision and consistency in school life. Unfortunately, the evidence for these judgements is not supplied, and a reading of school OFSTED reports leaves one with the impression that there are a limited number of performance indicators statements which are used to compile the reports, hopefully on the basis of team discussions of observed practice, expression of views and behaviour.

Into this arena fell the work of the National Forum on Values in Education and the Community, initiated by Nick Tate in 1996. It is indicative of the profile given to values in our education system that they were only given explicit curricular attention eight years after ERA. Yet the whole curriculum, the life of the school and the nature of teaching and learning which takes place is the context into which the national curriculum falls. I do not wish to catalogue or critique the workings of the Forum (of which I was a member) here, though I believe significant criticisms can be made about its processes (see Taylor, 1997b). One of the outcomes of the Forum is a statement of 'values' on society, relationships, self and the environment, which received the public endorsement of a MORI poll. Meanwhile the School Curriculum and Assessment Authority (SCAA), now the Qualifications and Curriculum Authority (QCA), has produced guidelines for SMSC, which are being piloted in 50 schools, with a view to indicating what must, ought and might be covered, possibly in a notional 5 per cent of Personal and Social Education (PSE) curriculum time in the revised curriculum frameworks for 2000. It is envisaged that case studies, a resource directory, a glossary and guidelines for community service will also be produced.

Such is the framework for values education in the state education system and its curricula which, in turn, form the arena for research. The irony is that much of this deliberation, policy making by government and its agencies as well as schools, and the endeavours of inspection and now curriculum developers, takes place in almost total ignorance of current intentions, practices and awareness at the school level. Due to the fact that the endorsement of values education has been largely rhetorical, and not, unlike other aspects of the national curriculum, resourced or researched, we know very little about school ideology, provision, implementation and outcomes in the values domain. Despite this lack of 'market research', schools are about to receive a more specific injection of curriculum input, and, no doubt, will be left to make of it what they will. One positive effect of the higher profile given to values education latterly, has, however, been to bring to the surface some conceptual and practical issues for values education in England, so, before focusing on current empirical research, I will briefly outline some of the more contentious points.

PHILOSOPHICAL RESEARCH INTO VALUES EDUCATION: SOME CONCEPTUAL AND PRACTICAL ISSUES

Research into values education is in many ways a daunting topic, partly because the terms 'research' and 'values education' are conceptually and culturally loaded. Research is mainly theoretical, empirical or applied. These types of research can be unpacked further; for example, empirical research – on which I shall concentrate later – can be quantitative, qualitative, experimental and so on. Each has a particular, distinctive and complementary body of evidence to contribute. The strength of theoretical, philosophical research – much needed in the values domain – is that it seeks to elucidate and clarify concepts and issues and may indicate ways forward. Of the conceptual and practical issues which abound in considering values education, I should like to pose some unanswered questions which I believe should not be overlooked in the flurry of curriculum activity. These relate to key areas of school experience: definition, aims, content, process, evaluation and review.

Definition

What are 'values'? What is 'values education'? The problem of the definition and naming of the 'values' domain reflects the conceptual and curricular confusion surrounding the area and has many implications for practice. In my view, the current debate about what to call this area of educational experience is indicative of the lack of coherence and coordinated leadership by the various government agencies concerned with curriculum policy, inspection and teacher training, which have largely ploughed different furrows and have failed to set coherent and deliverable goals. Thus we currently have several different labels for roughly the same domain of experience: Spiritual, Moral, Social and Cultural Development (SMSC) as OFSTED have it; Personal and Social Education (PSE) as most secondary schools call it; or Values Education, at least in SCAA's Forum mode, though QCA seems to be speaking more of PSE, or, increasingly, citizenship. Whilst I am unsure what's in a name, I am increasingly convinced that the 'values' domain, whatever called, is worthy of a specific timetabled place in the curriculum. OFSTED's definitions of SMSC still seem viable, and the moral area of experience is at least arguably distinctive in both content and form. Indeed, John Wilson made a good case for this 30 years ago! (Wilson, Williams and Sugarman, 1967). One of the problems with the idea of values education is that, as an umbrella term, it may be too unfocused. However, it *is* inclusive. The collection of papers, edited by Mark Halstead and myself (1996), set out the scope of values in education: spiritual, moral, environmental, democratic, aesthetic, health and so on. In the introduction Mark Halstead helpfully offered a definition of values as 'principles, fundamental convictions, ideals, standards or life stances which as general guides to behaviour or as points of reference in decision making or the evaluation of beliefs or action which are closely connected to personal integrity and personal identity' (p. 5). At the National Foundation for Educational Research (NFER) we have used this definition in slightly modified form in a research project surveying values in education in primary and secondary school; it seems to be a relevant term for the senior management respondents (Taylor and Lines, 1999).

Aims

A central issue, which does not seem to have adequate and specific attention at the national level, even if most schools have 'clear and well established aims' (OFSTED, 1997) is 'What are we aiming for in values education?' What does being prepared for the 'opportunities, responsibilities and experiences of adult life' imply when we consider that young people in school now will be facing the global and cyberspace challenges of the coming century? Though some of the policy documents quoted earlier may give hints, is education for citizenship, for example, to aim at law-abiding citizens, who mind their own business and who maintain the *status quo*; or who are participative, proactive members of society (all of them?); or who are citizens of the world with a global consciousness? To what extent is critical thinking to be applied to values? Moreover, are we only interested in individual development, or also that of institutions and groups? Answers to these kinds of questions relate firmly to the vision of the nature of society and world in which we wish to live.

Content

What values? Whose values? There has been much philosophical debate about whether there are shared values or core values. Earlier policy guidance forthrightly listed certain proscribed values of which schools should take note. However, as I have argued elsewhere (Taylor, 1996a) their implementation was clearly open to further articulation, perception and interpretation. What exactly is meant by 'acting considerately towards others' or 'dishonesty'? In the guided rush of the Forum to get consensus on values, the existence of this list seems to have been overlooked. But are the terms of the NCC 1993 discussion document (reissued by SCAA 1996) or those in the Forum's list actually *values?* I think schools have to be suspicious of lists of values because they are not neutral as to time or place. Values education is closely tied to the political development of a country, because every government emphasises different values. Education, which often appears to be in a process of more or less continuous reform, both influences and reflects social and ideological change, fashion and events; sometimes the thrust is on specific programmes of health, sex or drug education, at other times on bullying, next it may be parenting; gradually, there may be a move towards longer-term aspirations of developing a learning society or community. In this sense it is strange that the old issue of the extent to which values should be prescribed has raised its head here again. If there are commonly agreed values then why should schools pick and mix from them, on the rationalisation that school contexts and the issues which are pertinent to them are specific? Surely it is the fact that these values are commonly held which makes them universally valid to teach, irrespective of context. What I think is consistently missing is due acknowledgement of conflicts of value where there are serious, and possibly unresolvable, differences in values applications which stem from different world views. For example, some young people from minority cultural backgrounds have to reconcile conflicts of values in their daily living, but schools pay little attention to this process explicitly, or how such young people come to arrive at their own set of values.

Process

Several serious issues arise when we consider how values education should be delivered. How are the aims for values education to be achieved most effectively? Which kinds of methods lead to which outcomes? Is it to be a separately timetabled subject? Is there sufficient curriculum space? How is it that some secondary schools give priority to values education and have at least one period of PSE (or whatever it is called) when others have difficulty delivering values education in ten minutes of tutor time? The issue is not easily resolved, and in turn relates to the role and preparation of teachers. In practice, on the one hand, if values education is left to the cross-curricular themes, it may not be owned as the province of any teacher with expertise and may become so diluted as to be unrecognisable; on the other hand, if it becomes a separate area, delivered by specialists, then many teachers may consider themselves absolved.

This leads to other central questions: to what extent is every teacher a values educator? Do values come into every subject of the curriculum? Should the teacher of values be a neutral teacher? In policy guidance much seems to be made (at least by government) of the moral agency of teachers and the example they set. Is this how teachers see it? Observation suggests primary teachers are happier in this role than secondary teachers. Earlier OFSTED reports indicated that PSE was one of the most badly taught areas of the curriculum (OFSTED, 1995b). This is because teachers are rarely trained to handle controversial issues, and, while some relish it, others find it too personally and professionally challenging. Delivery is thus often dependent on the individual skills of the teacher. Much more attention is needed to consider how teachers can be empowered to deliver values education or PSE. What are teachers' views on this? Such questions seem to strike at the heart of the nature of teaching and learning and relate to the distinction which Richard Peters, the distinguished erstwhile Professor of Education of the Institute of Education, University of London, drew between the teacher being 'an authority' and 'in authority'. The teacher who may feel uncertain of his or her views or values may feel at a disadvantage if he/she feels expected to be an authority. But the teacher who has a confirmed view may also be at a disadvantage if his or her authority as a teacher is not respected. This refocuses on underlying questions about the moral standing of teachers and of the climate for learning. Can teachers be co-learners with their pupils? For example, if discussion is central to learning in values, what skills do they need to facilitate classroom talk?

Evaluation and review

Much is currently made of school self-evaluation and the capacity for self-renewal. Generally, however, teachers lack clear time for reflection about practice and this often has to be done at the chalk face. External agencies of various kinds can provide a stimulus by posing pertinent questions. Checklists, as in guidance documents, can help, as can the involvement of consultants and advisors. School inspections have galvanised not only the production of policies, but also more self-consciousness about, and evaluation of, practice. The need to produce follow-up action plans and school development plans has provided a structure for consideration of values issues and opportunities for offering more continuous planning and on-going review. Even so, there are indications that values curriculum audits are by no means commonplace and that progression and continuity of experience are fruitful grounds for further development. More specifically, the involvement of teachers in particular projects, such as trialling of curriculum materials in values, or even, dare one say it, in research exercises, can aid reflection. Being interviewed by a researcher in one's free period may not be lost time; a structured review can prompt awareness, recognition of strengths and weaknesses, and help to make meaning out of endeavours. Above all, it is important that evaluation and review are tailored to the aims and goals of the particular school, project, programme or activity.

Empirical research and school practice: some current work in England

Although many of the outstanding questions outlined above are issues for argument, debate and policy making at national and school levels, empirical research can provide some evidence from practice which begins to address them. Empirical research, even at the macro-level, on values in England has, until now, been sorely lacking. Indeed, there is a certain contrast to be drawn between the level of sponsored research in this domain in England and in Scotland. In respect of certain programme evaluation and micro-level research about certain aspects of moral development, work in North America is light years ahead.

In outlining some current research projects on aspects of values education, with which I am associated at the NFER, it may be worth briefly distinguishing certain functions of research and how they can help with policy formation and the development of school practice. Often a research project can serve several of these functions. This list is by no means comprehensive; for example, it does not include action research, which is not currently funded.

Information gathering

Much research at the macro-level is of this kind, whether it be the collection of data on on-going research, development and resources to form a directory (Taylor, 1994c), country reports and a comparative overview of practice in Europe (Taylor, 1994a), or basic data on provision in primary and secondary schools (Taylor, 1998; Taylor and Lines, 1999). Despite much public and educational debate about the state and status of values education in schools, little precise information exists about how schools approach values education, how their provision supports their stated values, why and how they choose certain curricular approaches and teaching strategies, and what professional support is needed. A project (sponsored by NFER, QCA and the Citizenship Foundation), has examined key factors in schools' formal and informal teaching in values education to provide evidence of coherent and interesting practice as a basis for policy-making and good practice guidelines. In particular, through an evaluation of the Citizenship Foundation's *'You, Me, Us'* (Rowe and Newton, 1994) materials for primary schools, the project has gained evidence of the kind of materials schools take up, use and find effective, as well as their resource and support needs (Taylor, Hill and Lines, 1998). Additionally, to inform the International Association for the Evaluation of Education Assessment (IEA) Civic Education Project, the project has surveyed secondary schools' provision for citizenship by the age of 15 (Kerr, 1998). The research involved a nationally representative questionnaire survey of 600 primary schools and 400 secondary schools; telephone interviews with up to 50 PSE coordinators; and mini case studies of around 20 primary and secondary schools. As you might suppose, the findings indicate a wide range of practice (see Taylor, 1998; Taylor and Lines, 1999).

Reports of such research can be used to inform other researchers, teacher trainers, schools and governments. They can also be used to raise awareness and lobby government agencies to be more proactive. Another research project being undertaken with Brian Gates (University College of St Martin, Lancaster) is part of this tradition. Current debate about values education in schools tends to overlook the need for teacher preparation to deliver a consistent and coherent curricular experience for pupils. To do this teachers require both initial training and continuing professional development. This collaborative research aims to build an up-to-date picture of teacher-training institutions offering moral education courses and the nature of these courses. A survey questionnaire will be sent to all teacher-training institutions in England and Wales. It will be followed up by telephone interviews and analysis of documentation. A report, setting the research data in the context of current national policy, will be produced.

Answering specific questions

Whilst there is a sense in which all research asks questions, whether it be by questionnaire or by interview in qualitative research, undertaking critical reviews of the research literature enables a focus on particular questions and the bringing to bear of a wide range of projects and their evidence. Such state-of-the-art reviews can be directed to specific questions to help teachers with decisions about school practice, as in the case of the review of research on values, attitudes and personal qualities, which Mark Halstead (University of Plymouth) and I have undertaken for OFSTED. Pupils' values and the role of schools in developing young people's attitudes and personal activities have come under greater scrutiny, both because of various horrific social acts perpetrated by children and because of renewed attention given to the provision for SMSC development in the Office for Standards in Education (OFSTED) inspections. This review of published research, in the UK and USA over the last ten years, aims, in relation to 5–16-year-olds, to: (a) clarify concepts and terminology; (b) consider the social context, non-school influences on young people's values, attitudes and personal qualities developed through school life (such as pro-social behaviour, caring, school democracy, rules and discipline, extra-curricular activities, teacher example); (c) aspects of the curriculum and teaching methods (all subjects, Religious Education and PSE, cross-curricular themes, circle time); and (d) as indicated in individual assessment and school evaluation. This overview of the state of the art in values education, will include an extensive bibilography and indicates further areas for research, curriculum development and school practice (Halstead and Taylor, 1999).

Critical reviews of research can also provide an overview of current policy and practice on certain themes or topics, such as civic education, which has been undertaken by my NFER colleague, David Kerr. The International Association for the Evaluation of Educational Achievement (IEA) is currently organising a Civic Education Project in 24 countries worldwide focusing on citizenship in secondary education. Phase I of the project, to which this English case study contributes, addresses three core areas: young people's knowledge of democracy; their sense of national identity; and their awareness of the disenfranchised and marginalised. The project has involved a review of policy and research literature, and interviews with a range of education professionals and 'opinion leaders', focusing on policy objectives, teaching strategies and materials and school-based activities in relation to the core questions as set out by the IEA. The work has been guided by a national expert panel. The report includes an introduction to civic education and annotated bibliography (Kerr, 1998).

Evaluation

Two other projects have evaluated curriculum materials development projects. One has focused on the take up and use of the Citizenship Foundation's materials for primary schools, *'You, Me, Us!'*. The other is Association of Christian Teachers' Cross-curricular Christianity (CHARIS) project (Taylor, 1997c). This evaluation is particularly interesting because it has taken place alongside the curriculum development process itself, which has been undertaken by teachers, and the materials have also been evaluated by other teachers undertaking classroom trials. Recent educational policy, guidance and inspection have given renewed prominence to SMSC development in all curricular subjects. The CHARIS project has produced classroom materials for English, Mathematics, French and German and Science at Key Stage 4, which aim to enhance SMSC development from a Christian perspective (Shortt and Farnell, 1997, 1998). A concurrent evaluation of the project, also sponsored by the Jerusalem Trust, has been undertaken to: provide information on project development and management, consider issues in the development and dissemination of materials, and assess the extent to which the project achieves its own aims for pupils' SMSC development and the take-up of materials in secondary schools. The evaluation has been conducted by means of documentary analysis; observation of writing teams, interviews with team members and project directors; visits to schools trialling the materials including teacher interviews, class observation, pupil group interviews; telephone interviews with editors and designers; attendance at and contribution to project management meetings.

WHAT DO WE KNOW AND WHAT DON'T WE KNOW FROM RESEARCH INTO VALUES EDUCATION? SOME PRELIMINARY POINTS

From my international involvement in research on various aspects of values education I offer some general reflections on the overall state of research before concluding with some key aspects for further research endeavours in England if we are serious about wanting to improve school provision and pupil outcomes.

The nature of research into values education

There seem to be some major gaps in the kind of research evidence available. On the one hand, there is some limited evaluation at the macro-level in various countries about policy on values education and its influence on school structures and curriculum allocation. On the other hand, there is for example, a great deal of research evidence at the micro-level about assessing individuals' stages of moral reasoning development. Yet there are relatively few studies which have set out to observe specific values education strategies and evaluate their outcomes, particularly in a classroom context. Basically, we have few clear ideas about what works for whom, when and why! Teachers wishing to decide what kind of strategy to choose to implement in their school to address a certain kind of problem, would not, at present, have clear grounds or evidence for choice based on pupil outcomes.

The status of research into values education

The values domain is complex and education in this area controversial. Yet it is difficult to escape the conclusion that at least part of the reason why our level of knowledge about how to do values education is so incomplete is because it has never received the attention it deserves in the formal curriculum. Neither has research in this domain received the on-going financial input needed to develop significant understanding over time. Whilst small-scale studies can help to build up a picture of institutional processes and outcomes, much more longitudinal research, evaluating and comparing the implementation of specific programmes, is required, considering the impact of teacher training, experimental and control groups, appropriate outcome measures for individuals and groups, and so on.

In my Editorial to the 25th anniversary issue of the *Journal of Moral Education,* on moral education from the twentieth into the twenty-first century, I suggested that moral-education research posed many unanswered questions and had produced some unquestioned answers (Taylor 1996b). I concluded that

> despite 25 years of reporting on moral education in this Journal and long-standing, world-wide traditions of moral education endeavours, we are –
> at least – unsure of the extent of what we know about moral education,
> how to do it and how we know when it has been successful. (p. 10)

Dwight Boyd (1996) also considered that 'the range of theory is a poor indicator for educational practice' and doubted that 'the field has yet developed to the point of permitting sound generalisations about empirical generalisations about practice' (p. 22). In my editorial I identified many gaps in research on moral education. Whilst that is only a small part of what is intended by the values domain, the points made have wide application. Indeed, the science of moral education is much more developed than certain other aspects of values education – spiritual education, for example. Despite this pessimistic conclusion, I shall review a few basic and broad findings from the overall pattern of research.

The role of the teacher

This is clearly a key factor in many ways, not just because the teacher is a mediator of the text, but because he/she is a person and in a personal learning relationship with the pupil. Elsewhere (Taylor, 1996c) I attempted to indicate some of the moral roles expected of teachers, at least in England. These comprise: exemplar, caregiver, counsellor, informer, facilitator, modeller, creator of a learning community, arbiter. In England, however, there is also some ambivalence. On the one hand, there is a not uncontentious expectation that teachers are 'moral agents who imply values by the way they address pupils and each other, the way they dress, the language they use and the effort they put into their work' (NCC, 1993, p. 8). On the other hand, there seems to be some recognition that teachers, particularly at secondary level, should be able to withdraw from teaching PSE as such, even though they are being encouraged to develop the values dimensions in their subject teaching. Given the significance of the teacher as a moral values educator, it is vital that the expectations be made clear and consistent if a more accurate assessment of teacher performance is to be attempted. Moreover, it goes without saying that, for values education to succeed, much more focused and on-going efforts for teachers' initial training and continuing professional development are imperative. At present, training in moral education is minimal: in short but obligatory components of courses, or as an optional specialism, and, only occasionally, as a separate course.

School strategies and processes

A conclusion from the OFSTED overview of research is that schools need to work on not just one but several strategies simultaneously. But they also need to be clear about what aims they intend and what effects are looked for from each strategy. Schools need a whole-school approach *and* a curriculum audit. In so doing they need to work out a coherent approach which offers progression and continuity in values education across the life of the school. There is a case for a distinctive course, in moral education, for some time, possibly, but not necessarily, in each year group. The values dimension of each subject area also needs unpacking, as it does in the cross-curricular themes. Curriculum content has to be forward looking to meet the needs of young people, the issues which are relevant to them (for example, drugs) and which will always be at the cutting edge in terms of personal and social moral challenges (for example, environmental issues). The curriculum thus needs to be predicting the values issues for the coming century, such as ethical use of genetic engineering and the possible redefinition of global morality because of cyberspace technology. The provision offered in the formal curriculum needs charting in relation to the experience of students in the informal or at worst contradictory.

Most importantly, attention needs to be given to processes and strategies. Discussion is a central plank of moral education. But it is not only the skills of talking and presenting an argument, and knowing relevant information, which are important, but also being able to listen, reflect, respond. The values dimensions of listening have yet to be researched. Yet the listening teacher is always recognised and conunended by pupils. Latterly dialogue has come more into prominence through narrative approaches, where meaning making occurs through the process of talk itself. At another level, dialogue is also important in communitarianism. Another neglected area is education of the emotions – what of moral imagination and courage? Too great a concentration on reasoning and other knowledge or skill-based approaches ignores the vital dispositions of will and determination.

Criteria for success

Should the focus really be on school provision or effects on pupils' values, attitudes, personal qualities and behaviour? What kind of outcomes are being looked for? These differ at the macro- and the micro-level of research. Research involving individual assessment on certain measures (for example, the Kohlberg's Moral Judgement Interview (MJI), Rest's Defining Issues Test, Gibbs' Sociomoral Reflection Objective Measure) focuses on statistically significant effects. These may be very different from educational effects. What does a statistical effect mean in terms of students' observable behaviour or attitudes? Indeed, very small statistical effect sizes may not be surprising, given that social values, beliefs and attitudes are very resistant to change. Moreover, in studies, for example, of moral reasoning development through class discussions, not all students develop, at the same rate, as measured by the MJI. Whilst attention has been given to improving validity of measures, rater reliability, and so on, teaching processes and relationships with teachers and peers have had far less scrutiny to see why what works for some does not work for others. Only now is the school effectiveness agenda beginning to consider what makes for an effective valuing, valued and values-educating school (Taylor, 1999).

A FURTHER RESEARCH AGENDA FOR VALUES EDUCATION

In concluding, it is appropriate to make some suggestions for future research (see also Taylor, 1996b).

- *Pay more attention to the general socio-political, economic, technological and cultural influences* surrounding values education, its profile, status and the aims and objectives set out for it as part of the political agenda of governments. How do schools set about interpreting these injunctions? How can they also promote ethical reflection on them?

- *Get much clearer about the specific goals of values education in a society or school* and what it would be to achieve them. Values, and especially moral education, is essentially about what kind of society we wish to live in. As Dwight Boyd (1996) has reminded us, over the past 25 years mainstream approaches to moral education have focused on the development of individuals and their interaction 'when it is arguably the relationship of group to group that forms the context for the most egregious moral problems of our times' (p. 29). Certain groups, such as ethnic minorities, have been marginalised from the values debate. Even where discussion about shared values or core values has begun it is still at a superficial level. Schools (and researchers) need to ask themselves: Do we need to be clearer about our aims and objectives for values education? Is there a shared understanding of what terms mean? How can we get all members of the school community involved? Are there agreed criteria for what is to count as a successful outcome? What targets can be set? What might performance indicators look like?

- *Take explicit and serious account of the informal influences on young people's values development* – family, friends, media. To educate in school without a clear awareness of parents' desires for the values education of their children, parents' own values, and a sense of the ways in which they operate in relation to their children's upbringing is to ignore more than half – and probably the more influential half – of the agencies which consciously intend to shape character, inform moral understanding, foster personal and social skills and transmit values. It is also particularly important to work with minority ethnic communities to enhance intercultural understanding. There is much need for research to explore to what extent schools have sought to develop genuine partnerships with parents in the values education of the young, not only in terms of such strategies as school–home contracts, but also in coming to an understanding of what parents want and expect schools to do, where parents and teachers see the boundaries between home and school influences, what is distinctive about the contributions of each, and how both can work more effectively in liaison and together to common purpose.

- *Find out what help teachers would like in delivering moral education.* Do teachers most need reflection, thus for planning, resources, consultative support, experience of working together? What are teachers' understandings of values concepts and how do they employ them in their teaching? What ideology influences their teaching style? How do they 'see' the ethical dimensions of teaching and professional life? We know very little about the answers to these questions.

- *Recognise and make use of everyday life as a values educator across the lifespan.* By focusing on values education in formal settings, or even in the home, we largely overlook the learning that takes place, if we care to reflect on events and behaviour in everyday life, at work, in the street and community, and so on. For instance, research by Krebs and colleagues (for example, Krebs and Denton, 1997) indicates that real-life moral decision making, is pragmatic, self-interested and geared towards desired outcomes. Whilst people may be motivated to behave in ways which are consistent with their moral principles they can also alter these to fit and justify the way they behave. At present we seem to know very little about how this ongoing moral learning occurs across the lifespan, though we are beginning to recognise that it may be accelerated or changed by critical life incidents. The special issue of the *Journal of Moral Education* in 1998 (Guest Editor, Mal Leicester) specifically investigated lifelong moral education. There is scope for much more research into values education across the lifespan. Formal values education in schools is only a starting point for the development of awareness, values, attitudes and skills and a preparation for moral behaviour in independent living. We need to value experience, rising to life's challenges, making moral meaning out of life and the ongoing development of a moral sense as an integral part of identity.

TO END – ANOTHER QUESTION AND A PLEA!

Are we capitalising on what we know from research when it comes to featuring values education in the life of the school and the curriculum? Even though at present we only have some general and rather imprecise answers, whilst we pursue various research undertakings might there not be value in raising further the profile of values education itself? If the recent attention given to values is not once again to be seen as mere rhetoric, then it requires that not only are the implications for resourcing and professional development taken seriously, but so is the function of a continuous body research to reflect and inform school practice.

REFERENCES

Boyd, D. (1996) 'A Question of Adequate Aims', *Journal of Moral Education*, 25 (1), 21–30.
Great Britain Statutes (1988) *Education Reform Act 1988.* London, HMSO.
Great Britain Statutes (1992) *Education (Schools) Act 1992.* London, HMSO, chapter 38.
Halstead, J. M. and Taylor, M. J. (eds) (1996), *Values in Education and Education in Values.* Lewes, Falmer Press.
Halstead, J. M. and Taylor, M. J. (1999) *The Development of Values, Attitudes and Personal Qualities.* A review of research (provisional title). London, OFSTED.
Kerr, D. (1998), 'Citizenship Education Revisited. National Case Study: England', in Torney-Purta, J. Schwille and J. A. Amadeo (eds), *Civic Education Across Countries: 22 Case Studies from the Civic Education Project.* Amsterdam, Eburon Publishers for the IEA.
Krebs, D. and Denton, K. (1997), 'The Forms and Functions of Real-life Moral Decision-making', *Journal of Moral Education*, 26 (2), 131–45.
National Curriculum Council (NCC) (1990a), 'The National Curriculum and Whole Curriculum Planning: Preliminary Guidance, Circular No. 6', York, NCC.
National Curriculum Council (1990b), 'Education for Citizenship, Curriculum Guidance 8', York, NCC.
National Curriculum Council (1993) 'Spiritual and Moral Development', Discussion Paper, York, NCC.
OFSTED (1994a) 'Spiritual, Moral, Social and Cultural Development', OFSTED Discussion Paper, London, OFSTED.
OFSTED (1994b) *Handbook for the Inspection of Schools.* London, HMSO.
OFSTED (1995a) *Framework for the Inspection of Nursery, Primary, Middle, Secondary*

and Special Schools. London, HMSO.

OFSTED (1995b) *The Annual Report of Her Majesty's Chief Inspector of Schools, Part I: Standards and Quality in Education.* London, HMSO.

OFSTED (1997) *The Annual Report of Her Majesty's Chief Inspector of Schools.* London, HMSO.

Rowe, D. and Newton, J. (1994) *You, Me, Us! Social and Moral Responsibility for Primary Schools.* London, The Citizenship Foundation.

Saunders, L., Hewitt, D. and MacDonald, A. (1995) *Education for Life: The Cross-curricular Themes in Primary and Secondary Schools.* Slough, NFER.

Shortt, J. and Farnell, A. (1997) *The Charis Project* (Charis English, Charis Mathematics, Charis Français and Charis Deutsch). St Albans, Association of Christian Teachers.

Shortt, J. And Farnell, A. (1998) *The Charis Project* (Charis English, Charis Mathematics, Charis Français, Charis Deutsch and Charis Science). Nottingham, The Stapleford Centre.

Taylor, M. J. (ed.) (1994a) *Values Education in Europe: A Comparative Overview of a Survey of 26 Countries in 1993.* Dundee, CIDREE and UNESCO.

Taylor, M. J. (1994b) 'England', *Values Education in Europe: A Comparative Overview of a Survey of 26 Countries in 1993.* Dundee, CIDREE and UNESCO.

Taylor, M. J. (1994c), *Values Education in the UK: A Directory of Research and Resources.* Slough, NFER.

Taylor, M. J. (1996a), 'Voicing Their Values: Pupils' Moral and Cultural Experience', in J. M. Halstead and M. J. Taylor (eds), *Values in Education and Education in Values.* Lewes, Falmer Press.

Taylor, M. J. (1996b), Editorial: 'Unanswered Questions, Unquestioned Answers', *Journal of Moral Education*, 25 (1), 5–20.

Taylor, M.J.(1996c), 'Values Education in Westem Europe: The Teacher's Role', *Mores*, 201, 19–27.

Taylor, M. J. (1997a) 'A Non-religious Response: Sharing in Dialogue From Diverse Sources', in J. Shortt and T. Cooling (eds), *Agenda for Educational Change.* Leicester, Apollos Press.

Taylor, M. J. (1997b) 'Shared Values: Valuing the Search', *The Quest for Common Values.* London, Interfaith Network.

Taylor, M. J. (1997c) 'Evaluation of the Association of Christian Teachers' Cross-Curricular Christianity Charis Project, Final Report', Report to the Trustees of the Jerusalem Trust (unpublished).

Taylor, M. J. (1998) *Values Education and Values in Education: A Guide to the Issues.* London, ATL.

Taylor, M. J. (1999) 'Values Education: Issues and Challenges in Policy and Practice', in M. Leicester, C. Modgil and S. Modgil (eds), *Values, Culture and Education, Vol. 2, Institutional Issues.* London, Cassell.

Taylor, M. J. and Lines, A. (1999) *Values Education in Primary and Secondary Schools.* Slough, NFER.

Taylor, M. J., Hill, C. and Lines, A. (1998) Evaluation of the Citizenship Foundation's Primary School Materials, *You, Me, Us!,* Final Report to the Citizenship Foundation (unpublished).

Wilson, J. B., Williams, N. and Sugarman, B. (1967) *An Introduction to Moral Education.* Harmondsworth, Penguin.

POSTSCRIPT:

CURRICULUM 2000 – THE MAY 1999 PROPOSALS FOR A REVISED NATIONAL CURRICULUM

Denis Lawton

All of the chapters in this book were written in connection with a conference that took place some time before the Labour government announced its proposals for a revision of the National Curriculum which had originally been designed (and re-designed) between 1988 and 1997 (that is, during the Thatcher/Major years).

Most, if not all, of the contributors to this book would agree that the 1999 revision *Curriculum 2000* is an improvement: it is less detailed, less prescriptive, gives some more autonomy to teachers and generally goes some way towards remedying many of the imperfections some contributors to this volume alluded to. But it is, I suggest, still not sufficiently forward-looking to last for more than the first few years of the twenty-first century. It is very good, from a values point of view that Personal, Social and Health Education, as well as Citizenship and Education for Democracy receive much more attention. The curriculum as a whole, however, is still dominated by an antiquated list of subjects and does not achieve the kind of balance that is necessary. Values are much discussed in the document but insufficient attention has been given to the problem of relating values to what is taught in classrooms, and the questions of relating pedagogy to a more enlightened school culture. The discussions about values contained in this volume will, therefore, continue for some years to come.

NOTES ON CONTRIBUTORS

Jo Cairns is Assistant Director at the Quality Assurance Agency.

The Most Reverend and Right Honourable Dr **George Carey** is Archbishop of Canterbury.

Robert Cowen is Reader in Comparative Education, Institute of Education, University of London.

Roy Gardner is Senior Lecturer in Education Institute of Education, University of London.

Denis Lawton is Professor of Education at the Institute of Education, University of London.

David Morrison is Professor of Canadian Studies and of Religious Studies, University of Prince Edward Island, Canada.

Richard Pring is Professor of Education and Director of the Department of Educational Studies, University of Oxford.

Marianne Talbot is Lecturer in Philosophy, Brasenose College, Oxford.

Nick Tate is Director of the Qualifications and Curriculum Authority.

Monica Taylor is Senior Research Officer, National Foundation of Educational Research.

Paddy Walsh is Senior Lecturer in Education, Institute of Education, University of London.

Babara Wintersgill is Her Majesty's Inspector, at the Office for Standards in Education.

INDEX